Warren Buffett
Talks to MBA Students

Warren Buffett

CONTENTS:

Buffett Lecture at the University of Florida School of Business.

October 15, 1998.

This speech was the first in a series sponsored by the Graham-Buffett Teaching

Endowment, established in 1997 by a $1 million gift from (1970 UF graduate) Mason Hawkins.

Introduction

The Graham-Buffett Course sequence is important to this college because it enables us to attract students who want this perspective on investing and managing corporations—a perspective that has been successfully employed by Mr. Buffett, Mr. Hawkins, and before them, Benjamin Graham.

This perspective is quite simple but is sometimes lost in the complexity of our university analysis. The perspective is that you have to understand the underlying economics of the businesses that you invest in, work in. You have to be clear-eyed and not be swayed by the crowd or passing fancies of the moment. And you have to learn and stick to disciplined principles of business valuation.

In the long run this disciplined approach will more often than not bring success, or more importantly avoid spectacular failures.

Hopefully, at the University of Florida we can successfully convey those principles and create a program for the very best students, and in time, the very best employers as well.

We thank Mr. Hawkins for his gift ($1 million) and share his thoughts today.

Mason Hawkins: He is someone I have admired tremendously for the last 30 years. In addition, he is someone each of us could pattern our lives after as a role model. It is my honor to introduce our lifetime's best long-term investor.

Buffett: (Holds mike) Testing: One million $, two million $…three million $.

I would like to say a few words primarily, and then the highlight for me will be getting your questions. I want to talk about what is on your mind.

Your Future

I would like to talk for just one minute to the students about your future when you leave here because you will learn a tremendous amount about investments; you all have the ability to do well; you all have the IQ to do well. You all have the energy and initiative to do well or you wouldn't be here. Most of you will succeed in meeting your aspirations.

But in determining whether you succeed there is more to it than intellect and energy. I would like to talk just a second about that. In fact, there was a guy, Pete Kiewit in Omaha, who used to say he looked for three things in hiring people: integrity, intelligence, and energy. And he said if the person did not have the first two, the later two would kill him because if they don't have integrity, you want them dumb and lazy. We want to talk about the first two because we know you have the last two. You are all second-year MBA students, so you have gotten to know your classmates. Think for a moment that I granted you the right to buy 10% of one of your classmate's earnings for the rest of their lifetime. You can't pick someone with a rich father; you have to pick someone who is going to do it on his or her own merit. And I gave you an hour to think about it.

Will you give them an IQ test and pick the one with the

highest IQ? I doubt it. Will you pick the one with the best grades? The most energetic? You will start looking for qualitative factors, in addition to (the quantitative) because everyone has enough brains and energy. You would probably pick the one you responded the best to, the one who has the leadership qualities, the one who is able to get other people to carry out their interests. That would be the person who is generous, honest and who gave credit to other people for their own ideas. All types of qualities. Whomever you admire the most in the class. Then I would throw in a hooker. In addition to this person, you had to go short one of your classmates.

That is more fun. Who do I want to go short? You wouldn't pick the person with the lowest IQ, you would think about the person who turned you off, the person who is egotistical, who is greedy, who cuts corners, who is slightly dishonest.

As you look at those qualities on the left and right-hand side, there is one interesting thing about them. It is not the ability to throw a football 60 yards; it is not the ability the run the 100-yard dash in 9.3 seconds; it is not being the best-looking person in the class. They are all qualities that if you really want to have the ones on the left-hand side, you can have them.

They are qualities of behavior, temperament, character that are achievable; they are not forbidden to anybody in this group. And if you look at the qualities on the right-hand side, the ones that turn you off in other people, there is not a quality there that you have to have. You can get rid of it. You can get rid of it a lot easier at your age than at my age because most behaviors are habitual. The chains of habit are too light to be felt until they are too heavy to be broken. There is no question about it. I see people with these self-destructive behavior patterns at my age or even twenty years younger and they really are entrapped by them.

They go around and do things that turn off other people right and left. They don't need to be that way but by a certain point they get so they can hardly change it. But at your age you can have any habits, any patterns of behavior that you wish. It is simply a question of which you decide.

Ben Graham looked around at the people he admired and Ben Franklin did this before him. Ben Graham did this in his low teens and he looked around at the people he admired and he said, "I want to be admired, so why don't I behave like them?" And he found out that there was nothing impossible about behaving like them. Similarly he did the same thing on the reverse side in terms of getting rid of those qualities.

I would suggest is that if you write those qualities down and think about them a while and make them habitual, you will be the one you want to buy 10% of when you are all through. And the beauty of it is that you already own 100% of yourself and you are stuck with it. So you might as well be that person, that somebody else.

Well, that is a short little sermon. So let's get on with what you are interested in. Let's start with questions...

Question: What about Japan? Your thoughts about Japan?

Buffett: My thoughts about Japan? I am not a macro guy. Now I say to myself:

Berkshire Hathaway can borrow money in Japan for 10 years at one percent. One percent! I say, gee, I took Graham's class 45 years ago and I have been working hard at this all my life; maybe I can earn more than 1% annually, it doesn't seem impossible. I wouldn't want to get involved in currency risk, so it would have to be Yen-denominated. I would have to be in Japanese Real Estate or Japanese companies or something of the sort and all I have to do is beat one percent. That is all the money is going to cost me and I can get it for 10 years. So far I haven't found anything. It is kind of interesting. The Japanese businesses earn very low returns on equity - 4% to 5% - 6% on equity, and it is very hard to earn a lot as an investor when the business you are in doesn't earn very much money.

Now some people do it. In fact, I have a friend, Walter Schloss, who worked at Graham at the same time I did. And it was the first way I went at stocks, to buy stocks selling way below working capital. A very cheap, quantitative approach to stocks. I call it the cigar butt approach to investing. You walk down the street and you look around for a cigar butt someplace. Finally you see one and it is soggy and kind of repulsive, but there is one puff left in it. So you pick it up and the puff is free—it is a cigar butt stock. You get one free puff on it and then you throw it away and try another one. It is not elegant. But it works. Those are low return businesses.

But time is the friend of the wonderful business; it is the enemy of the lousy business. If you are in a lousy business for a long time, you will get a lousy result even if you buy it cheap. If you are in a wonderful business for a long time, even if you pay a little bit too much going in, you will get a wonderful result if you stay in a long time. I find very few wonderful businesses in Japan at present. They may change the culture in some way so that management gets more shareholder responses over there and stock returns are higher. At the present time you will find a lot of low return businesses, and that was true even when the Japanese economy was booming. It is amazing; they had an incredible market without incredible companies. They were incredible in terms of doing a lot of business, but they were not incredible in terms of the return on equity that they achieved and that has finally caught up with them. So we have so far done nothing there.

But as long as money is 1% there, we will keep looking.

Question: You were rumored to be one of the rescue buyers of Long Term Capital. What was the play there? What did you see?

Buffett: The Fortune Magazine that has Rupert Murdoch on the cover. It tells the whole story of our involvement; it is kind of an interesting story. I got the really serious call about LTCM on a Friday afternoon that things were getting serious. I know those people most of them pretty well—most of them at Salomon when I was there. And the place was imploding and the FED was sending people up that weekend, between that Friday and the following Wednesday when the NY Fed, in effect, orchestrated a rescue effort, but without any Federal money involved. I was quite active but I was having a terrible time reaching anybody.

We put in a bid on Wednesday morning. I talked to Bill McDonough at the NY Fed. We made a bid for 250 million for the net assets but we would have put in 3 and 3/4 billion on top of that. Three billion dollars from Berkshire, $700 million from AIG, and $300 million from Goldman Sachs. And we submitted that but we put a very short time limit on that because when you are bidding on 100 billion worth of securities that are moving around, you don't want to leave a fixed price bid out there for very long.

In the end the bankers made the deal, but it was an interesting period. The whole LTCM is really fascinating because if you take Larry Hillenbrand, Eric Rosenfeld, John Meriwether and the two Nobel prize winners—if you take the 16 of them, they have about as high an IQ as any 16 people working together in one business in the country, including Microsoft; an incredible amount of intellect in one room. Now you combine that with the fact that those people had extensive experience in the field they were operating in. These were not a bunch of guys who had made their money selling men's clothing and all of a sudden went into the securities business. They had in aggregate, the 16 had 300 or 400 years of experience doing exactly what they were doing; and then you throw in the third factor that most of them had most of their very substantial net worth's in the businesses—hundreds and hundreds of millions of their own money up (at risk), super-high intellect, and working in a field that they knew. Essentially they went broke. That to me is absolutely fascinating.

If I ever write a book it will be called, "Why Smart People Do Dumb Things." My partner says it should be autobiographical. But this might be an interesting illustration. They are perfectly decent guys. I respect them and they helped me out when I had problems at Salomon. They are not bad people at all. But to make money they didn't have and didn't need, they risked what they did have and what they did need. That is just plain foolish; it doesn't matter what your IQ is. If you risk something that is important to you for something that is unimportant to you it just doesn't make sense. I don't care if the odds you succeed are 99 to 1 or 1000 to 1 that you succeed. If you hand me a gun with a million chambers with one bullet in a chamber and put it up to your temple and I am paid to pull the trigger, it doesn't matter how much I would be paid. I would not pull the trigger. You can name any sum you want, but it doesn't do anything for me on the upside and I think the downside is fairly clear. Yet people do it financially very much without thinking.

There was a lousy book with a great title written by Walter Gutman—"You Only Have to

Get Rich Once." Now that seems pretty fundamental. If you have $100 million at the beginning of the year and you will make 10% if you are unleveraged, and 20% if you are leveraged 99 times out of a 100, what difference if at the end of the year, you have $110 million or $120 million? It makes no difference. If you die at the end of the year, the guy who makes up the story may make a typo, he may have said 110 even though you had a 120. You have gained nothing at all. It makes absolutely no difference. It makes no difference to your family or anybody else.

The downside, especially if you are managing other people's money, is not only losing all your money, but it is disgrace, humiliation and facing friends whose money you have lost. Yet 16 guys with very high IQs entered into that game. I think it is madness. It is produced by an over-reliance to some extent on things. Those guys would tell me back at Salomon; a six Sigma event wouldn't touch us. But they were wrong. History does not tell you of future things happening. They had a great reliance on mathematics. They thought that the Beta of the stock told you something about the risk of the stock. It doesn't tell you a damn thing about the risk of the stock in my view.

Sigma's do not tell you about the risk of going broke in my view, and maybe now in their view too. But I don't like to use them as an example. The same thing in a different way could happen to any of us where we really have a blind spot about something that is crucial because we know a whole lot of something else. It is like Henry Kauffman said:

"The ones who are going broke in this situation are of two types: the ones who know nothing and the ones who know everything." It is sad in a way.

I urge you. We basically never borrow money. I never borrowed money even when I had $10,000 basically, what difference did it make. I was having fun as I went along it didn't matter whether I had $10,000 or $100,000 or $1,000,000 unless I had a medical emergency come along.

I was going to do the same things when I had a little bit of money as when I had a lot of money. If you think of the difference between me and you, we wear the same clothes basically (SunTrust gives me mine), we eat similar food— we all go to McDonald's or better yet, Dairy Queen, and we live in a house that is warm in winter and cool in summer. We watch the Nebraska (football) game on big screen TV. You see it the same way I see it. We do everything the same—our lives are not that different. The only thing we do is we travel differently. What can I do that you can't do?

I get to work in a job that I love, but I have always worked at a job that I loved. I loved it just as much when I thought it was a big deal to make $1,000. I urge you to work in jobs that you love. I think you are out of your mind if you keep taking jobs that you don't like because you think it will look good on your resume. I was with a fellow at Harvard the other day who was taking me over to talk. He was 28, and he was telling me all he had done in life, which was terrific. And then I said, "What will you do next?" "Well," he said, "Maybe after I get my MBA I will go to work for a consulting firm because it will look good on my resume." I said, "Look, you are 28 and you have been doing all these things, you have a resume 10 times than anybody I have ever seen. Isn't that a little like saving up sex for your old age? "

There comes a time when you ought to start doing what you want. Take a job that you love. You will jump out of bed in the morning. When I first got out of Columbia Business School, I wanted to go to work for Graham immediately, for nothing. He thought I was over-priced. But I kept pestering him. I sold securities for three years and I kept writing him and finally I went to work for him for a couple of years. It was a great experience. But I always worked in a job that I loved doing. You really should take a job that if you were independently wealthy that would be the job you would take. You will learn something, you will be excited about, and you will jump out of bed. You can't miss. You may try something else later on, but you will get way more out of it and I don't care what the starting salary is.

When you get out of here take a job you love, not a job you think will look good on your resume. You ought to find something you like.

If you think you will be happier getting 2x instead of 1x, you are probably making a mistake. You will get in trouble if you think making 10x or 20x will make you happier because then you will borrow money when you shouldn't or cut corners on things. It just doesn't make sense and you won't like it when you look back.

Question: What makes a company something that you like?

Buffett: I like businesses that I can understand. Let's start with that. That narrows it down by 90%. There are all types of things I don't understand, but fortunately, there is enough I do understand. You have this big wide world out there and almost every company is publicly owned, so you have all American business practically available to you, so it makes sense to go with things you can understand. I can understand this, anyone can understand this (Buffett holds up a bottle of Coca-Cola). Since 1886, it is a simple business, but it is not an easy business—I don't want an easy business for competitors. I want a business with a moat around it. I want a very valuable castle in the middle and then I want the Duke who is in charge of that castle to be very honest and hardworking and able. Then I want a moat around that castle. The moat can be various things: The moat around our auto insurance business, Geico, is low cost.

People have to buy auto insurance so everyone is going to have one auto insurance policy per car basically. I can't sell them 20, but they have to buy one. I can sell them one. What are they going to buy it on? (Based on what criteria?) They (customers) will buy based on service and cost. Most people will assume the service is identical among companies or close enough. So they will do it on cost. So I have to be a low-cost producer—that is my moat. To the extent that my costs are further below the other guy, I have thrown a couple of sharks into the moat. All the time you have this wonderful castle, there are people out there who are going to attack it and try to take it away from you. I want a castle I can understand, but I want a castle with a moat around it.

Kodak

30 years ago, Eastman Kodak's moat was just as wide as Coca-Cola's moat. I mean, if you were going to take a picture of your six-month-old baby and you want to look at that picture 20 years from now or 50 years from now. And you are never going to get a chance—you are not a professional photographer—so you can evaluate what is going to look good 20 or 50 years ago. What is in your mind about that photography company (Share of Mind) is what counts because they are promising you that the picture you take today is going to be terrific 20 to 50 years from now about something that is very important to you. Well, Kodak had that in spades 30 years ago; they owned that. They had what I call share of mind. Forget about share of market—share of mind. They had something—that little yellow box—that said Kodak is the best. That is priceless. They have lost some of that. They haven't lost it all.

It is not due to George Fisher. George is doing a great job, but they let that moat narrow.

They let Fuji come and start narrowing the moat in various ways. They let them get into the Olympics and take away that special aspect that only Kodak was fit to photograph the Olympics. So Fuji gets there and immediately in people's minds, Fuji becomes more into parity with Kodak.

You haven't seen that with Coke; Coke's moat is wider now than it was 30 years ago. You can't see the moat day by day, but every time the infrastructure that gets built in some country that isn't yet profitable for Coke that will be 20 years from now. The moat is widening a little bit. Things are all the time changing a little in one direction or the other. Ten years from now, you will see the difference. Our managers of the businesses we run, I have one message to them, and we want to widen the moat. We want to throw crocs, sharks and gators into the moat to keep away competitors. That comes about through service, through quality of product; it comes about through cost, sometimes through patents, and/or real estate location. So that is the business I am looking for.

Now what kind of businesses am I going to find like that? Well, I am going to find them in simple products because I am not going to be able to figure what the moat is going to look like for Oracle, Lotus or Microsoft ten years from now. Gates is the best businessman I have ever run into, and they have a hell of a position, but I really don't know what that business is going to look like ten years from now. I certainly don't know what his competitors will look like ten years from now. I know what the chewing business will look like ten years from now. The Internet is not going to change how we chew gum and nothing much else is going to change how we chew gum. There will lots of new products. Is Spearmint or Juicy Fruit going to evaporate? It isn't going to happen. You give me a billion dollars and tell me to go into the chewing gum business and try to make a real dent in Wrigley's. I can't do it. That is how I think about businesses. I say to myself, give me a billion dollars and how much can I hurt the guy? Give me $10 billion dollars and how much can I hurt Coca-Cola around the world? I can't do it. Those are good businesses.

Now give me some money and tell me to hurt somebody in some other fields, and I can figure out how to do it.

So I want a simple business, easy to understand, great economics now, honest and able management, and then I can see about in a general way where they will be ten years from now. If I can't see where they will be ten years from now, I don't want to buy it. Basically, I don't want to buy any stock where if they close the NYSE tomorrow for five years, I won't be happy owning it. I buy a farm and I don't get a quote on it for five years and I am happy if the farm does OK. If I buy an apartment house and don't get a quote on it for five years, I am happy if the apartment house produces the returns that I expect. People buy a stock and they look at the price next morning and they decide to see if they are doing well or not doing well. It is crazy. They are buying a piece of the business. That is what Graham—the most fundamental part of what he taught me.

You are not buying a stock; you are buying part ownership in a business. You will do well if the business does well, if you didn't pay a totally silly price. That is what it is all about. You ought to buy businesses you understand. Just like if you buy farms, you ought to buy farms you understand. It is not complicated.

Incidentally, by the way, in calling this Graham-Buffett, this is pure Graham. I was very fortunate. I picked up his book ("The Intelligent Investor") when I was nineteen. I got interested in stocks when I was six or seven. I bought my first stock when I was eleven. But I was playing around with all this stuff—I had charts and volume and I was making all types of technical calculations and everything. Then I picked up a little book that said you are not just buying some little ticker symbol that bounces around every day; you are buying part of a business. Soon as I started thinking about it that way, everything else followed. It is very simple. So we buy businesses we think we can understand. There is no one here who can't understand Coke...

If I was teaching a class at business school, on the final exam I would pass out the information on an Internet company and ask each student to value it. Anybody that gave me an answer, I'd flunk. (Laughter)

I don't know how to do it. But people do it all the time; it is more exciting. If you look at it like you are going to the races—that is a different thing—but if you are investing... Investing is putting out money to be sure of getting more back later at an appropriate rate.

And to do that you have to understand what you are doing at any time. You have to understand the business. You can understand some businesses but not all businesses.

Question: You covered half of it, which is trying to understand a business and buying a business. You also alluded to getting a return on the amount of capital invested in the business. How do you determine what is the proper price to pay for the business?

Buffett: It is a tough thing to decide, but I don't want to buy into any business I am not terribly sure of. So if I am terribly sure of it, it probably won't offer incredible returns. Why should something that is essentially a cinch to do well offer you 40% a year? We don't have huge returns in mind, but we do have in mind not losing anything. We bought See's Candy in 1972. See's Candy was then selling 16 m. pounds of candy at a $1.95 a pound, and it was making 2 bits a pound or $4 million pre-tax. We paid $25 million for it—6.25 x pretax or about 10x after tax. It took no capital to speak of. When we looked at that business—basically, my partner, Charlie, and I—we needed to decide if there was some <u>untapped pricing power</u> there, where that $1.95 box of candy could sell for $2 to $2.25. If it could sell for $2.25 or another $0.30 per pound, that was $4.8 on 16 million pounds, which on a $25 million purchase price was fine. We never hired a consultant in our lives; our idea of consulting was to go out and buy a box of candy and eat it.

What we did know was that they had share of mind in California. There was something special. Every person in California has something in mind about See's Candy and overwhelmingly it was favorable. They had taken a box on Valentine's Day to some girl and she had kissed him. If she slapped him, we would have no business. As long as she kisses him, that is what we want in their minds. See's Candy means getting kissed. If we can get that in the minds of people, we can raise prices. I bought it in 1972, and every year I have raised prices on Dec. 26th, the day after Christmas, because we sell a lot on Christmas. In fact, we will make $60 million this year. We will make $2 per pound on 30 million pounds.

Same business, same formulas, same everything—$60 million bucks and it still doesn't take any capital.

And we make more money 10 years from now. But of that $60 million, we make $55 million in the three weeks before Christmas. And our company song is: "What a friend we have in Jesus." (Laughter) It is a good business. Think about it a little. Most people do not buy boxed chocolate to consume themselves; they buy them as gifts—somebody's birthday or more likely it is a holiday. Valentine's Day is the single biggest day of the year. Christmas is the biggest season by far. Women buy for Christmas and they plan ahead and buy over a two or three-week period. Men buy on Valentine's Day. They are driving home; we run ads on the radio. Guilt, guilt, guilt—guys are veering off the highway right and left. They won't dare go home without a box of chocolates by the time we get through with them on our radio ads. So that Valentine's Day is the biggest day.

Can you imagine going home on Valentine's Day—our See's Candy is now $11 a pound, thanks to my brilliance. And let's say there is candy available at $6 a pound. Do you really want to walk in on Valentine's Day and hand—she has all these positive images of See's Candy over the years—and say, "Honey, this year I took the low bid." And hand her a box of candy. It just isn't going to work. So in a sense, there is <u>untapped pricing power</u>—it is not price dependent.

Think of Disney. Disney is selling Home Videos for $16.95 or $18.95 or whatever. All over the world, people—and we will speak particularly about Mothers in this case—have something in their mind about Disney. Everyone in this room, when you say Disney, has something in their mind about Disney. When I say Universal Pictures, if I say 20th Century Fox, you don't have anything special in your mind. Now if I say Disney, you have something special in your mind. That is true around the world.

Now picture yourself with a couple of young kids, whom

you want to put away for a couple of hours every day and get some peace of mind. You know if you get one video, they will watch it twenty times. So you go to the video store or wherever to buy the video. Are you going to sit there and premier 10 different videos and watch them each for an hour and a half to decide which one your kid should watch? No. Let's say there is one there for $16.95 and the Disney one for $17.95—you know if you take the Disney video that you are going to be OK. So you buy it. You don't have to make a quality decision on something you don't want to spend the time to do. So you can get a little bit more money if you are Disney and you will sell a lot more videos. It makes it a wonderful business. It makes it very tough for the other guy.

How would you try to create a brand—Dreamworks is trying—that competes with Disney around the world and replaces the concept that people have in their minds about Disney with something that says Universal Pictures? So a mother is going to walk in and pick out a Universal Pictures video in preference to a Disney. It is not going to happen.

Coca-Cola is associated with people being happy around the world, everyplace—Disneyland, the World Cup, the Olympics—where people are happy. Happiness and Coke go together. Now you give me—I don't care how much money—and tell me that I am going to do that with RC Cola around the world and have five billion people have a favorable image in their mind about RC Cola. You can't get it done. You can fool around; you can do what you want to do. You can have price discounts on weekends. But you are not going to touch it. That is what you want to have in a business. That is the moat. You want that moat to widen.

If you are See's Candy, you want to do everything in the world to make sure that the experience basically of giving that gift leads to a favorable reaction. It means what is in the box; it means the person who sells it to you because all of our business is done when we are terribly busy. People come in during those weeks before Christmas, Valentine's

Day, and there are long lines. So at five o'clock in the afternoon some woman is selling someone the last box candy and that person has been waiting in line for maybe 20 or 30 customers. And if the salesperson smiles at that last customer, our moat has widened, and if she snarls at them, our moat has narrowed. We can't see it, but it is going on every day. But it is the key to it. It is the total part of the product delivery. It is having everything associated with it; say See's Candy and something pleasant happening. That is what business is all about.

Question: If you have every bought a company where the numbers told you not to, how much is quantitative and how much is qualitative?

Buffett: The best buys have been when the numbers almost tell you not to because then you feel so strongly about the product and not just the fact you are getting a used cigar butt cheap. Then it is compelling. I owned a windmill company at one time. Windmills are cigar butts, believe me. I bought it very cheap. I bought it at a third of working capital. And we made money out of it, but there is no repetitive money to be made on it. There is a one-time profit in something like that. And it is just not the thing to be doing. I went through that phase. I bought streetcar companies and all kinds of things. In terms of the qualitative, I probably understand the qualitative the moment I get the phone call. Almost every business we have bought has taken five or ten minutes in terms of analysis.

We bought two businesses this year.

General Re is an $18 billion deal. I have never been to their home office. I hope it is there. (Laughter) There could be a few guys there saying, what numbers should we send Buffett this month? I could see them going once a month and saying we have $20 billion in the bank instead of $18 billion. I have never been there.

Before I bought Executive Jet, which is fractional ownership of jets, before I bought it, I had never been there. I bought my family a quarter-interest in the program three years earlier. And I have seen the service and it seems to develop well. And I got the numbers. But if you don't know enough to know about the business instantly, you won't know enough in a month or in two months. You have to have sort of the background of understanding and knowing what you do or don't understand. That is the key. It is defining your circle of competence.

Everybody has got a different circle of competence. The important thing is not how big the circle is, the important thing is the size of the circle; the important thing is staying inside the circle. And if that circle only has 30 companies in it out of thousands on the big board, as long as you know which 30 they are, you will be OK. And you should know those businesses well enough so you don't need to read lots of work. Now, I did a lot of work in the earlier years just getting familiar with businesses, and the way I would do that is use what Phil Fisher would call the "Scuttlebutt Approach." I would go out and talk to customers, suppliers, and maybe ex-employees in some cases. Everybody.

Every time I was interested in an industry, say it was coal, I would go around and see every coal company. I would ask every CEO, "If you could only buy stock in one coal company that was not your own, which one would it be and why? You piece those things together, you learn about the business after a while.

Funny, you get very similar answers as long as you ask about competitors. If you had a silver bullet and you could put it through the head of one competitor, which competitor would it be, and why? You will find who the best guy is in the industry. So there are a lot of things you can learn about a business. I have done that in the past on the business I felt I could understand so I don't have to do that anymore. The nice thing about investing is that you don't have to learn

26

anything new. You can do it if you want to, but if you learn Wrigley's chewing gum forty years ago, you still understand Wrigley's chewing gum. There are not a lot of great insights to get of the sort as you go along. So you do get a database in your head.

I had a guy, Frank Rooney, who ran Melville for many years; his father-in-law died and had owned H.H. Brown, a shoe company. And he put it up with Goldman Sachs. But he was playing golf with a friend of mine here in Florida and he mentioned it to this friend, so my friend said "Why don't you call Warren?" He called me after the match and in five minutes I basically had a deal.

But I knew Frank, and I knew the business. I sort of knew the basic economics of the shoe business, so I could buy it. Quantitatively, I have to decide what the price is. But you know, that is either yes or no. I don't fool a lot around with negotiations. If they name a price that makes sense to me, I buy it. If they don't, I was happy the day before, so I will be happy the day after without owning it.

Question: The Asian Crisis and how it affects a company like Coke that recently announced their earnings would be lower in the fourth quarter.

Buffett: Well, basically I love it because the market for Coca-Cola products will grow far faster over the next twenty years internationally than it will in the United States. It will grow in the U.S. on a per capita basis. The fact that it will be a tough period for—who knows? Three months or three years—but it won't be tough for twenty years. People will still be going to be working productively around the world and they are going to find this is a bargain product in terms of a portion of their working day that they have to give up in order to have one of these—better yet, five of them a day like I do.

This is a product that in 1936 when I first bought six of those for a quarter and sold them for a nickel each. It was in a 6.5 oz bottle and you paid a two cents deposit on the bottle. That was a 6.5 oz. bottle for a nickel at that time; it is now a 12 oz. can which if you buy it on weekends or if you buy it in bigger quantities, so much money doesn't go to packaging— you essentially can buy the 12 ozs. for not much more than 20 cents. So you are paying not much more than twice the per oz. price of 1936. This is a product that has gotten cheaper and cheaper relative to people's earning power over the years and which people love. And in 200 countries, you have the per capita consumption use going up every year for a product that is over 100 years old that dominates the market. That is unbelievable.

One thing that people don't understand is one thing that makes this product worth tens and tens of billions of dollars is one simple fact about really all colas, but we will call it Coca-Cola for the moment. It happens to be a name that I like. Cola has no taste memory. You can drink one of these at 9 o'clock, 10 o'clock, 1 o'clock and 5 o'clock.

The one at 5 o'clock will taste as good to you as the one you drank early in the morning. You can't do that with Cream Soda, Root Beer, Orange, Grape. All of those things accumulate on you. Most foods and beverages accumulate; you get sick of them after a while. And if you eat See's Candy—we get these people who go to work for us at See's Candy and the first day they go crazy, but after a week they are eating the same amount as if they were buying it, because chocolate accumulates on you. There is no taste memory to Cola, and that means you get people around the world who will be heavy users—who will drink five a day, or for Diet Coke, 7 or even 8 a day. They will never do that with other products. So you get this incredible per capita consumption. The average person in this part of the world or maybe a little north of here drinks 64 ozs. of liquid a day. You can have 64 ozs. of that be Coke and you will not get fed up with Coke if you like it to start with in the least. But if you do that with anything else, if you eat just one product all day, you will get a little sick of it after a while.

It is a huge factor. So today over 1 billion of Coca-Cola product servings will be sold in the world and that will grow year by year. It will grow in every country virtually, and it will grow on a per capita basis. And twenty years from now it will grow a lot faster internationally than in the U.S., so I really like that market better because there is more growth there over time. But it will hurt them in the short term right now, but that doesn't mean anything. Coca-Cola went public in 1919; the stock sold for $40 per share. The Chandler family bought the whole business for $2,000 back in the late 1880s. So now he goes public in 1919, $40 per share. One year later it is selling for $19 per share. It has gone down 50% in one year. You might think it is some kind of disaster and you might think sugar prices increased and the bottlers were rebellious and a whole bunch of things. You can always find reasons that weren't the ideal moment to buy it. Years later you would have seen the Great Depression, WWII and sugar rationing and thermonuclear weapons and the whole thing—there is always a reason.

But in the end, if you had bought one share at $40 per share and reinvested the dividends, it would be worth $5 million now ($40 compounding at 14.63% for 86 years!). That factor so overrides anything else. If you are right about the business you will make a lot of money. The timing part of it is very tricky thing so I don't worry about any given event if I got a wonderful business what it does next year or something of the sort. Price controls have been in this country at various times and that has fouled up even the best of businesses. I wouldn't be able to raise prices Dec 31st on See's Candy, but that doesn't make it a lousy business if that happens to happen because you are not going to have price controls forever. We had price controls in the early '70s.

The wonderful business—you can figure what will happen; you can't figure out when it will happen. You don't want to focus too much on when but you want to focus on what.

If you are right about what, you don't have to worry about when very much.

Question: What about your business mistakes?

Buffett: How much time do you have? The interesting thing about investments for me and my partner, Charlie Munger— the biggest mistakes have not been mistakes of commission, but of omission. They are where we knew enough about the business to do something and where, for one reason or another, sat there sucking our thumbs instead of doing something. And so we have passed up things where we could have made billions and billions of dollars from things we understood, forget about things we don't understand. The fact I could have made billions of dollars from Microsoft doesn't mean anything because I never could understand Microsoft. But if I can make billions out of healthcare stocks, then I should make it. And I didn't when the Clinton health care program was proposed and they all went in the tank. We should have made a ton of money out of that because I could understand it.

I should have made a ton of money out of Fannie Mae back the mid-1980s, but I didn't do it. Those are billion-dollar mistakes or multi-billion dollar mistakes that generally accepted accounting principles don't pick up. The mistakes you see. I made a mistake when I bought US Air Preferred some years ago. I had a lot of money around. I make mistakes when I get cash. Charlie tells me to go to a bar instead. Don't hang around the office. But I hang around the office and I have money in my pocket, I do something dumb. It happens every time. So I bought this thing. Nobody made me buy it. I now have an 800 number I call every time I think about buying a stock in an airline. I say, "I am Warren and I am an air-aholic." They try to talk me down, "Keep talking. Don't do anything rash." Finally I got over it. But I bought it. And it looked like we would lose all our money in it. And we came very close to losing all our money in it. You can say we deserved to lose our money it.

We bought it because it was an attractive security, but it was not in an attractive industry. I did the same thing in Salomon. I bought an attractive security in a business I wouldn't have bought the equity in. So you could say that is one form of mistake: buying something because you like the terms, but you don't like the business that well. I have done that in the past and will probably do that again. The bigger mistakes are the ones of omission. Back when I had $10,000 I put $2,000 of it into a Sinclair Service Station which I lost, so the opportunity cost on that money is about $6 billion right now—fairly big mistakes. It makes me feel good when my Berkshire goes down because the cost of my Sinclair Station goes down too. My 20% opportunity cost. I will say this: it is better to learn from other people's mistakes as much as possible. But we don't spend any time looking back at Berkshire. I have a partner, Charlie Munger; we have been pals for forty years—never had an argument. We disagree on things a lot but we don't have arguments about it.

We never look back. We just figure there is so much to look forward to that there is no sense thinking of what we might have done. It just doesn't make any difference. You can only live life forward. You can learn something perhaps from the mistakes, but the big thing to do is to stick with the businesses you understand. So if there is a generic mistake outside your circle of competence like buying something that somebody tips you on or something of the sort, in an area you know nothing about, you should learn something from that, which is to stay with what you can figure out yourself. You really want your decision making to be by looking in the mirror. Saying to yourself, "I am buying 100 shares of General Motors at $55 because…" It is your responsibility if you are buying it. There's got to be a reason, and if you can't state the reason, you shouldn't buy it. If it is because someone told you about it at a cocktail party—not good enough. It can't be because of the volume or a reason like the chart looks good. It has to be a reason to buy the business. That we stick to pretty carefully. That is one of the things Ben Graham taught me.

Question: The current tenuous economic situation and interest rates? Where are we going?

Buffett: I don't think about the macro stuff. What you really want to in investments is figure out what is important and knowable. If it is unimportant and unknowable, you forget about it. What you talk about is important, but in my view, it is not knowable. Understanding Coca-Cola is knowable or Wrigley's or Eastman Kodak. You can understand those businesses that are knowable. Whether it turns out to be important depends where your valuation leads you and the firm's price and all that. But we have never not bought or bought a business because of any Macro feeling of any kind because it doesn't make any difference. Let's say in 1972, when we bought See's Candy, I think Nixon put on the price controls a little bit later, but so what! We would have missed a chance to buy something for $25 million that is producing $60 million pre-tax now. We don't want to pass up the chance to do something intelligent because of some prediction about something we are no good on anyway. So we don't read or listen to in relation to macro factors at all. The typical investment counselor organization goes out and they bring out their economist and they trot him out and he gives you this big macro picture.

And they start working from there on down. In our view that is nonsense.

If Alan Greenspan was on the one side of me and Robert Rubin on the other side and they both were whispering in my ear exactly what they were going to do the next twelve months, it wouldn't make any difference to me what I would pay for Executive Jet or General Re or anything else I do.

Question: What is the benefit of being an out-of-towner as opposed to being on Wall Street?

Buffett: I worked on Wall Street for a couple of years and I have my best friends on both coasts. I like seeing them.

I get ideas when I go there. <u>But the best way to think about investments is to be in a room with no one else and just think.</u> And if that doesn't work, nothing else is going to work. The disadvantage of being in any type of market environment like Wall Street in the extreme is that you get over-stimulated. You think you have to do something every day. The Chandler family paid $2,000 for this company (Coke). You don't have to do much else if you pick one of those. And the trick then is <u>not</u> to do anything else. Even not to sell at 1919, which the family did later on. So what you are looking for is some way to get one good idea a year and then ride it to its full potential, and that is very hard to do in an environment where people are shouting prices back and forth every five minutes and shoving reports in front of your nose and all that. Wall Street makes its money on activity. You make your money on inactivity.

If everyone in this room trades their portfolio around every day with every other person, you will all end up broke. And the intermediary will end up with all the money. If you all own stock in a group of average businesses and just sit here for the next 50 years, you will end up with a fair amount of money and your broker will be broke. He is like the doctor who gets paid on how often to get you to change pills. If he gave you one pill that cures you the rest of your life, he would make one sale, one transaction and that is it. But if he can convince you that changing pills every day is the way to great health, it will be great for him and the prescriptionists. You won't be any healthier and you will be a lot worse off financially. You want to stay away from any environment that stimulates activity. And Wall Street would have the effective of doing that.

When I went back to Omaha, I would go back with a whole list of companies I wanted to check out and I would get my money's worth out of those trips, but then I would go back to Omaha and think about it.

Question: How to evaluate Berkshire or MSFT if it does not pay dividends?

Buffett: It won't pay any dividends either. That is a promise I can keep. All you get with Berkshire, you stick it in your safe deposit box and then every year you go down and fondle it. You take it out and then you put it back. There is enormous psychic reward in that. Don't underestimate it.

The real question is if we can retain dollar bills and turn them into more than a dollar at a decent rate. That is what we try to do. And Charlie Munger and I have all our money in it to do that. That is all we will get paid for doing. We won't take any options or we won't take any salaries to speak of. But that is what we are trying to do. It gets harder all the time. The more money we manage the harder it is to do that. We would do way better percentage wise with Berkshire if it was 1/100th the present size. It is run for its owners, but it isn't run to give them dividends because so far every dollar that we earned or could have paid out, we have turned into more than a dollar. It is worth more than a dollar to keep it. Therefore, it would be silly to pay it out. Even if everyone was tax-free that owned it, it would have been a mistake to pay dividends at Berkshire because so far the dollar bills retained have turned into more than a dollar. But there is no guarantee that happens in the future. At some point the game runs out on that. That is what the business is about. Nothing else about the business do we judge ourselves by. We don't judge it by the size of its home office building or anything the like the number of people working there. We have 12 people working at headquarters and 45,000 employees at Berkshire, 12 people at HQ and 3,500 sq ft. and we won't change it.

But we will judge ourselves by the performance of the company, and that is the only way we will get paid. But believe me, it is a lot harder than it used to be.

Question: What tells you when an investment has reached its full potential?

Buffett: I don't buy Coke with the idea it will be out of gas in 10 years or 50 years. There could be something that happens but I think the chances are almost nil. So what we really want to do is buy businesses that we would be happy to own forever. It is the same way I fell about people who buy Berkshire. I want people who buy Berkshire to plan to hold it forever. They may not for one reason or the other but I want them at the time they buy it to think they are buying a business they are going to want to own forever.

And I don't say that is the only way to buy things. It is just the group to join me because

I don't want to have a changing group all the time. I measure Berkshire by how little activity there is in it. If I had a church and I was the preacher and half the congregation left every Sunday, I wouldn't say, "It is marvelous to have all this liquidity among my members; terrific turnover..." I would rather go to church where all the seats are filled every Sunday by the same people. Well, that is the way we look at the businesses we buy. We want to buy something virtually forever. And we can't find a lot of those. And back when I started, I had way more ideas than money, so I was just constantly having to sell what was the least attractive stock in order to buy something I just discovered that looked even cheaper. But that is not our problem really now. So we hope we are buying businesses that we are just as happy holding five years from now as now. And if we ever found a huge acquisition, then maybe we would have to sell something. Maybe to make that acquisition but that would be a very pleasant problem to have.

We never buy something with a price target in mind. We never buy something at 30 saying, if it goes to 40 we'll sell it, or 50 or 60 or 100. We just don't do it that way, anymore than when we buy a private business like See's Candy for

$25 million. We don't ever say, if we ever get an offer of $50 million for this business we will sell it. That is not the way to look at a business.

The way to look at a business is, is this going to keep producing more and more money over time? And if the answer to that is yes, you don't need to ask any more questions.

Questions: How did you decide to invest in Salomon?

Buffett: Salomon, like I said, I went into that because it was a 9% security in 1987, in

September 1987, and the Dow was up 35% and we sold a lot of stuff. And I had a lot of money around and it looked to me like we would never get to do anything, so I took an attractive security form in a business I would never buy the common stock of. I went in because of that, and I think generally it is a mistake. It worked out OK finally on that, but it is not what I should have been doing. I either should have waited, in which case I could have bought more Coca-Cola a year later or thereabouts, or I should have even bought Coke at the prices it was selling at even though it was selling at a pretty good price at the time. So that was a mistake.

On Long-Term Capital—we have owned other businesses associated with securities over the years—one of them is arbitrage. I've done arbitrage for 45 years and Graham did it for 30 years before that. That is a business unfortunately I have to be near a phone for. I have to really run it (arbitrage operations) out of the office myself because it requires being more market-attuned because I don't want to do that anymore. So unless a really big arbitrage situation came along that I understood, I won't be doing much of that. But I've probably participated in about 300 arbitrage situations at least in my life, maybe more. It was a good business, a perfectly good business.

LTCM has a bunch of positions, they have tons of positions, but the top ten are probably 90% of the money that is at risk, and I know something about those ten positions. I don't know everything about them by a long shot, but I know enough that I would feel OK at a big discount going in and we had the staying power to hold it out. We might lose money on something on that, but the odds are with us. That is a game that I understand. There are few other positions we have that are not that big because they can't get that big. But they could involve yield curve relationships or on the run-off the run governments that are just things you learn over time being around securities markets. They are not the base of our business. Probably on average, they have accounted for ½ - ¾ a percentage point of our return a year. They are little pluses you get for actually having been around a long time.

Arbitrage

One of the first arbitrages I did involved a company that offered cocoa beans in exchange for their stock. That was in 1955. I bought the stock, turned in the stock, got warehouse certificates for cocoa beans, and they happened to be a different type but there was a basis differential and I sold them. That was something I was around at the time, so I learned about it. There hasn't been a cocoa deal since—40 odd years I have been waiting for a cocoa deal. I haven't seen it. It is there in my memory if it ever comes along. LTCM is that on a big scale.

Question: Diversification?

Buffett: The question is about diversification. I have a dual answer to that. If you are not a professional investor, if your goal is not to manage money to earn a significantly better return than the world, then I believe in extreme diversification. I believe 98% - 99% who invest should extensively diversify and not trade, so that leads them to an index fund type of decision with very low costs. All they are going to do is own part of America, and they have made a decision that owning a part of America is worthwhile. I don't quarrel with that at all. That is the way they should approach it unless they want to bring an intensity to the game to make a decision and start evaluating businesses. Once you are in the businesses of evaluating businesses and you decide that you are going to bring the effort and intensity and time involved to get that job done, then I think diversification is a terrible mistake to any degree. I got asked that question the other day at SunTrust. If you really know businesses, you probably shouldn't own more than six of them.

If you can identify six wonderful businesses, that is all the diversification you need. And you will make a lot of money. And I can guarantee that going into a seventh one instead of putting more money into your first one is going to be a terrible mistake. Very few people have gotten rich on their seventh best idea. But a lot of people have gotten rich with their best idea. So I would say for anyone working with normal capital who really knows the businesses they have gone into, six is plenty, and I probably have half of what I like best.

I don't diversify personally. All the people I've known that have done well with the exception of Walter Schloss—Walter diversifies a lot. I call him Noah; he has two of everything.

Question: How do you distinguish the Cokes of the world from the Proctor & Gambles of this world?

Buffett: Well, P&G is a very, very good business with strong distribution capability and lots of brand names, but if you ask me and I am going to go away for twenty years and put all my family's net worth into one business, would I rather have P&G or Coke? Actually, P&G is more diversified among product line, but I would feel more sure of Coke than P&G. I wouldn't be unhappy if someone told me I had to own P&G during the twenty-year period. I mean, that would be in my top 5 percent. Because they are not going to get killed, but I would feel better about the unit growth and pricing power of a Coke over twenty or thirty years.

Right now the pricing power might be tough, but you think a billion servings a day for a penny each or $10 million per day. We own 8% of that, so that is $800,000 per day for Berkshire Hathaway. You could get another penny out of the stuff. It doesn't seem impossible. I think it is worth a penny more. Right now it would be a mistake to try and get it in most markets. But over time, Coke will make more per serving than it does now. Twenty years from now I guarantee they will make more per serving, and they will be selling a whole lot more servings. I don't know how many or how much more, but I know that.

P&G's main products—I don't think they have the kind of dominance, and they don't have the kind of unit growth, but they are good businesses. I would not be unhappy if you told me that I had to put my family's net worth into P&G and that was the only stock I would own. I might prefer some other name, but there are not 100 other names I would prefer.

Question: Would you buy McDonald's and go away for twenty years?

Buffett: McDonald's has a lot of things going for it, particularly abroad, again. Their position abroad in many countries is stronger than it is here. It is a tougher business over time. People don't want to be eating—exception to the kids when they are giving away beanie babies or something—at McDonald's every day. If people drink five Cokes a day, they probably will drink five of them tomorrow. The fast food business is tougher than that, but if you had to pick one hand to have in the fast food business, which is going to be a huge business worldwide, you would pick McDonald's. I mean, it has the strongest position.

It doesn't win taste test with adults. It does very well with children and it does fine with adults, but it is not like it is a clear winner. And it is gotten into the game in recent years of being more price promotional—you remember the experiment a year ago or so. It has gotten more dependent on that rather than selling the product by itself. I like the product by itself. I feel better about Gillette if people buy the Mach 3 because they like the Mach

3 than if they get a Beanie Baby with it. So I think fundamentally it is a stronger product if that is the case. And that is probably the case.

We own a lot of Gillette, and you can sleep pretty well at night if you think of a couple billion men with their hair growing on their faces. It is growing all night while you sleep. Women have two legs; it is even better. So it beats counting sheep. And those are the kinds of business you look for. But what type of promotion am I going to put out there against Burger King next month, or what if they sign up Disney and I don't get Disney? I like the products that stand alone absent price promotion or appeals, although you can build a very good business based on that. And McDonald's is a terrific business. It is not as good a business as Coke. There really hardly are any. It is a very good business, and if you bet on one company in that field bet on McDonald's. We bought Dairy Queen a while back that is why I am plugging it shamelessly here.

Question: What do you think about the utility industry?

Buffett: I have thought about that a lot because you can put big money in it. I have even thought of buying the entire businesses. There is a fellow in Omaha, actually, that has done a little of that through Cal Energy. But I don't quite understand the game in terms of how it is going to develop with deregulation. I can see how it destroys a lot of value through the high-cost producer once they are not protected by a monopoly territory.

I don't for sure see who benefits and how much. Obviously, the guy with very low cost power or some guy who has hydro-power at two cents a kw has a huge advantage. But how much of that he gets to keep or how extensively he can send that outside his natural territory, I haven't been able to figure that out, so I really know what the industry will look like in ten years. But it is something I think about, and if I ever develop any insights that call for action, I will act on them. Because I think I can understand the attractiveness of the product—all the aspects of certainty of users' need and the fact it is a bargain and all of that. I understand. I don't understand who is going to make the money in ten years, and that keeps me away.

Question: Why do large caps outperform small caps (1998)?

Buffett: We don't care if a company is large cap, small cap, middle cap, micro cap. It doesn't make any difference. The only questions that matter to us:

• Do we understand the business?

• Do we like the people running it?

• And does it sell for a price that is attractive?

From my personal standpoint, running Berkshire now because we got pro-forma for Gen. Re, $75 to $80 billion to invest in, and I only want to invest in five things, so I am really limited to very big companies. But if I were investing $100,000, I wouldn't care whether something was large cap or small cap or anything. I would just look for businesses I understood.

Now, I think on balance, large cap companies as businesses have done extraordinarily well the last ten years—way better than people anticipated they would do. You really have American businesses earning close to something 20% on equity. And that is something nobody dreamed of and that is being produced by very large companies in aggregate. So you have had this huge revaluation upwards because of lower interest rates and much higher returns on capital. If American business is really a disguised bond that earns 20%, a 20% coupon, it is much better than a bond with a 13% coupon, and that has happened with big companies in recent years; whether it is permanent or not is another question. I am skeptical of that. I wouldn't even think about it—except for questions of how much money we run—I wouldn't even think about the size of the business. See's Candy was a $25 million business when we bought it. If I can find one now as big as we are, I would love to buy it. It is the certainty of it that counts.

Question: The securitization of real estate?

Buffett: There has been enormous securitization of the debt also of real estate, and that is one of the items right now that is really clogging up the capital markets. The mortgage back securities are just not moving—commercial, not residential mortgage backs. But I think you are directing your question at equities probably. The equities, if you leave out the corporate form, have been a lousy way to own equities. You have interjected a corporate income tax into something that people individually have been able to own with a single tax, and to have the normal corporate form you have a double taxation in there. You really don't need it and it takes too much of the return.

REITS have, in effect, created a conduit so you don't get the double taxation, but they also generally have fairly high operating expenses. If you get real estate, let's just say you can buy fairly simple types of real estate at an 8% yield, or thereabouts, and you take away close to 1% to 1.5% by the time you count stock options and everything, it is not a terribly attractive way to own real estate. Maybe the only way a guy with a $1,000 or $5,000 can own it, but if you have $1 million or $10 million, you are better off owning the real estate properties yourself instead of sticking some intermediary in between who will get a sizable piece of the return for himself. So we have found very little in that field.

You will see an announcement in the next couple of weeks that may belie what I am telling you today. I don't want you to think I am double-crossing you up here. But generally speaking, we have seen very little in that field that gets us excited. People sometimes get very confused about it—they will look at some huge land company, like Texas Pacific Land Trust, which has been around over 100 years and has got a couple of million acres in Texas, and they will sell 1% of their land every year and they will take that and come up with some huge value compared to the market value. But that is nonsense if you really own the property. You can't move. You can't move 50% of the properties or 20% of the properties; it is way worse than an illiquid stock. So you get these, I think, you get some very silly valuations placed on a lot of real estate companies by people who really don't understand what it is like to own one and try to move large quantity of properties.

REITS have behaved horribly in this market, as you know, and it is not at all inconceivable that they become a class that would get so unpopular that they would sell at significant discounts from what you could sell the properties for. And they could get interesting as a class, and then the question is whether management would fight you in that process because they would be giving up their income stream for managing things, and their interests might run counter to the shareholders on that. I have always wondered about REITS that have managements; they say their assets are so wonderful and they are so cheap, and then they (management) go out and sell stock. There is a contradiction in that.

They say, our stock is very cheap at $28, and then they sell a lot of stock at $28 less an underwriting commission. There is a disconnect there. But it is a field we look at.

Charlie and I can understand real estate, and we would be open for very big transactions periodically. If there was a LTCM situation translated to real estate, we would be open to that. The trouble is so many other people would be too that it would unlikely go at a price that would get us really get us excited.

Question: A down market is good for you?

Buffett: I have no idea were the market is going to go. I prefer it going down, but my preferences have nothing to do with it. The market knows nothing about my feelings. That is one of the first things you have to learn about a stock. You buy 100 shares of General Motors (GM). Now all of a sudden you have this feeling about GM. It goes down, you may be mad at it. You may say, "Well, if it just goes up for what I paid for it, my life will be wonderful again." Or if it goes up, you may say how smart you were and how you and GM have this love affair. You have got all these feelings. The stock doesn't know you own it.

The stock just sits there; it doesn't care what you paid or the fact that you own it. Any feeling I have about the market is not reciprocated. I mean, it is the ultimate cold shoulder we are talking about here. Practically anybody in this room is probably more likely to be a net buyer of stocks over the next ten years than they are a net seller, so every one of you should prefer lower prices. If you are a net eater of hamburger over the next ten years, you want hamburger to go down unless you are a cattle producer. If you are going to be a buyer of Coca-Cola and you don't own Coke stock, you hope the price of Coke goes down. You are looking for it to be on sale this weekend at your supermarket. You want it to be down on the weekends not up on the weekends when you tend the supermarket.

The NYSE is one big supermarket of companies. And you are going to be buying stocks. What do you want to have happen? You want to have those stocks go down, way down; you will make better buys then. Later on, twenty or thirty years from now when you are in a period when you are dis-saving, or when your heirs dis-save for you, then you may care about higher prices. There is Chapter 8 in Graham's

"Intelligent Investor" about the attitude toward stock market fluctuations—that and Chapter 20 on the Margin of Safety are the two most important essays ever written on investing, as far as I am concerned.

Because when I read Chapter 8 when I was 19, I figured out what I just said; it is obvious, but I didn't figure it out myself. It was explained to me. I probably would have gone another 100 years and still thought it was good when my stocks were going up. We want things to go down, but I have no idea what the stock market is going to do. I never do and I never will. It is not something I think about at all.

When it goes down, I look harder at what I might buy that day because I know there is more likely to be some merchandise there to use my money effectively in.

Moderator: OK, Warren, we will let you take one more question from the audience...

Buffett: I will let you pick who get it. You can be the guy... (Laughter)

Question: What would you do to live a happier life if you could live over again?

Buffett: This will sound disgusting. The question is, how would I live my life over again to live a happier life? The only thing would be to select a gene pool where people lived to 120 or something where I came from.

I have been extraordinarily lucky. I mean, I use this example, and I will take a minute or two because I think it is worth thinking about a little bit. Let's just assume it was 24 hours before you were born and a genie came to you and he said, "Herb, you look very promising and I have a big problem. I got to design the world in which you are going to live in. I have decided it is too tough; you design it. So you have twenty-four hours. You figure out what the social rules should be, the economic rules and the governmental rules, and you and your kids and their kids will live under those rules.

You say, "I can design anything? There must be a catch." The genie says there is a catch. You don't know if you are going to be born black or white, rich or poor, male or female, infirm or able-bodied, bright or retarded. All you know is you are going to take one ball out of a barrel with 5.8 billion (balls). You are going to participate in the ovarian lottery. And that is going to be the most important thing in your life because that is going to control whether you are born here or in Afghanistan or whether you are born with an IQ of 130 or an IQ of 70. It is going to determine a whole lot. What type of world are you going to design?

I think it is a good way to look at social questions because not knowing which ball you are going to get, you are going to want to design a system that is going to provide lots of goods and services because you want people on balance to live well. And you want it to produce more and more so your kids live better than you do and your grandchildren live better than their parents. But you also want a system that does produce lots of goods and services that does not leave behind a person who accidentally got the wrong ball and is not well wired for this particular system. I am ideally wired for the system I fell into here. I came out and got into something that enables me to allocate capital—nothing so wonderful about that. If all of us were stranded on a desert island somewhere and we were never going to get off of it, the most valuable person there would be the one who could raise the most rice over time. I can say, "I can allocate capital!" You wouldn't be very excited about that. So I have been born in the right place.

Gates says that if I had been born three million years ago, I would have been some animal's lunch. He says, "You can't run very fast, you can't climb trees, you can't do anything." You would just be chewed up the first day. You are lucky; you were born today. And I am. The question, getting back:

here is this barrel with 6.5 billion balls, everybody in the world; if you could put your ball back, and they took out at random a 100 balls and you had to pick one of those, would you put your ball back in?

Now, those 100 balls you are going to get out, roughly 5 of them will be American, 95/5. So if you want to be in this country, you will only have 5 balls, half of them will be women and half men—I will let you decide how you will vote on that one. Half of them will below average in intelligence and half above average in intelligence. Do you want to put your ball in there? Most of you will not want to put your ball back to get 100. So what you are saying is: I am in the luckiest one percent of the world right now sitting in this room—the top one percent of the world. Well, that is the way I feel. I am lucky to be born where I was because it was 50 to 1 in the United States when I was born. I have been lucky with parents, lucky with all kinds of things, and lucky to be wired in a way that in a market economy pays off like crazy for me. It doesn't pay off as well for someone who is absolutely as good a citizen as I am (by) leading Boy Scout troops, teaching Sunday school, or whatever, raising fine families, but just doesn't happen to be wired in the same way that I am. So I have been extremely lucky so I would like to be lucky again.

Then the way to do it is to play out the game and do something you enjoy all your life and be associated with people you like. I only work with people I like. If I could make $100 million dollars with a guy who causes my stomach to churn, I would say no because in way that is very much like marrying for money, which is probably not a very good idea in any circumstances, but if you are already rich, it is crazy. I am not going to marry for money. I would really do almost exactly what I have done except I wouldn't have bought the US Air.

Thank you.
END

Buffett speaks at Columbia

On Thursday evening (5/9/02), Columbia Business School's Seminar on Value Investing welcomed Warren Buffett as the guest speaker. I was lucky enough to worm my way into it. Here are my notes. (I don't claim that everything is completely accurate, but I think I captured at least the proper meaning of everything).

5:55 pm: Five minutes to go. The classroom looks like it was built to hold about 160 students and currently holds about 200 people—mainly students, with a few suit-and-tie types sprinkled in. There is some excitement, but not as much as the Berkshire annual meeting I went to two years ago. It was an interesting dynamic: In Omaha, everyone there made an effort to be there, which resulted in almost everyone knowing a good deal about Buffett and having some familiarity. In the classroom, there was a bit more curiosity, a "Do you think he'll have bodyguards?" kind of thing. I take my seat in the back and notice three cans of cherry coke lined up on the front table.

6:05 pm: Buffett walks in, picks up a can of cherry coke and holds it aloft. Everyone laughs. Bruce Greenwald acts as moderator. After a couple of class-related announcements, I get my first surprise—Walter Schloss is here, too. "If Warren Buffett can be thought of as the Babe Ruth of value investing, then Walter Schloss is the Ty Cobb and Satchel Paige combined." He notes Schloss' longevity—47 years of remarkable performance. [Prompted by Buffett later on, Schloss claims a 20.9% (pre-fees) annual return over that time period.]

Greenwald then notes how peculiar it feels to be responsible for introducing someone who clearly needs no introduction. He identifies Warren Buffett as "The Rose Blumkin of the investment world." Buffett takes the microphone—"Testing, one billion, two billion."

Some early remarks:

Speaking on the longevity brought up with regard to Schloss, Buffett knows what he wants people to be saying at his funeral: "My God, he was old!"

Notes that he has now been married for 50 years and 3 weeks, and says that being married to Susie is "the only thing that's happened better than taking Graham's class." He then points to Susie, who is sitting in the front row (surprise number two). [I think that Carol Loomis and Peter Buffett were also there, but I'm not positive.]

Next, the questions, which he leaves open to anything, whether business or personal related. As anyone who's ever seen Buffett speak can tell you, the questions were pretty standard. What makes the presentation interesting is the path that Buffett's answers take. Throughout this question-and-answer period, which lasts slightly over two hours, WEB is on his feet, leaning back onto a table, cherry coke at his side.

1. Options – We know you don't like them, but what about the companies you own?

WEB only knows of 2 companies that expense options (as is allowed under SFAS 123, but not practiced by many, for obvious reasons): Boeing and Winn-Dixie. He notes that a company (in Manhattan?) is currently voting on switching to an expensing convention. In most cases, options don't do a great job of providing the right incentives. Of all the employees in Berkshire Hathaway, Gen Re employees have made more, by far, from options in the last couple of years than anyone else in BRK. Looking at the dismal results of

Gen Re indicates how capricious option rewards can be.

For BRK specifically, it doesn't make sense to give options to anyone. Anything that a division/subsidiary manager does to influence results is swamped by wiggles in the overall portfolio of businesses. Compensation arrangements at BRK are created and agreed upon in minutes—no consultants needed.

Across the spectrum, compensation plans are crazy.

WEB has an envelope with the name of his successor. (The first thing this note says is "Check my pulse again.") It makes sense for him to have options—he would be responsible for the overall business. However, two critical features of these options would be:

- They would be granted with an exercise price equal to the greater of intrinsic value or market value.

- They would include a cost of capital effect so that the exercise price would be increasing each year.

As generally done, options are terrible. There's nothing inherently wrong with options. In the Buffett Limited Partnership, he had options: 25% of any returns in excess of 6%. However, he drew no salary and those options included a cost of capital.

2. Will the Wall Street Journal erode their moat with their recent cosmetic changes [moving a little towards USA Today]?

WSJ is an interesting case. 30 years ago, Dow Jones & Co. owned the world with regard to financial information. They had no competition to speak of. Most newspapers at that time defined their population by geography. The WSJ editor built the circulation from 50,000 to 1.5 million by defining population by interest. Their population had amazing demographics.

Over the past 30 years, financial information has been a growth industry. Dow Jones missed the boat. Their business was taken away by CNBC and Bloomberg. They got very self-satisfied. In 15 years, they went from number two on Fortune's "Most Admired Companies" list to about number 200.

He compared it to Classic Coke vs. New Coke. In the 1980s, Pepsi was conducting their "Pepsi Challenge" across America—and winning. People at Coke wouldn't admit it, but in 1985, Pepsi was driving them buggy. Americans will always go for a sweeter product in a taste test. Pepsi simply had [has] more calories than Coke and was [is] sweeter. So Coke decided to add some sweetness/calories to compete. They tested New Coke across 300,000 people in every conceivable demographic slice before they brought it out. Pepsi capitalized on New Coke by calling the introduction of New Coke a product recall of Old Coke. Pepsi actually declared a holiday in their company on that day and took out ads the day before the formal New Coke release: "The other guy just blinked."

As it turns out, the mystique of the Coke formula is great. Only two people know it; it is locked in a Sun Trust vault, etc., etc. In reality, Coke can make Pepsi and Pepsi can make Coke. You can break down the formula. At one point, Pepsi was moving towards introducing a product called Savannah Cola, which was equal in formula to the Old Coke. The only problem they faced was that one of the ingredients from the formula was hard to obtain because almost the entire production was purchased by the Coca Cola Company. Little by little, they were able to obtain this ingredient and were within two weeks of bringing it out when Coke relented and made Classic Coke.

[Talk about how important the "feelings" are with Coke, and the associations one has when thinking about Coke: the fact that he could say RC Cola and no one would have much of a response, but he could say Coke and every single one of us would have some type of reaction. Pepsi consistently beat Coke in a blind challenge. New Coke consistently beat Old Coke in a blind challenge. Yet for some reason, people went ballistic when Coke changed the formula. That's how embedded the Coke idea is.]

It's like See's Candy. It's not that well known in the East, but 33 million people in California will all have a reaction to the See's name. When people in California put a piece of See's Candy in their mouth, they like it a lot. When you tell them that it's See's, they like it even more. It's the combination of all the thoughts that go into the experience.

The Coke CEO a couple of years ago got into trouble when he spoke of a vending machine that could vary prices depending on the weather, increasing prices in hot weather. [WEB: At least say it in a way like you are lowering prices in cold weather...] That brought a lot of bad feelings with it. When you're making $0.01 per 8 oz. serving and serving over 1 billion of those servings every single day, that's $4 billion in earnings per year—all because of $0.01 per serving. It's critical, huge to keep a favorable opinion in people's minds.

3. Concerning the comment about a nuclear attack made at the annual meeting—how is BRK insurance adapting?

BRK is writing probably more terrorism insurance than anyone else. Amazingly, it is almost all being sold with NCB (nuclear, chemical, and biological warfare) exclusion. A few policies have been sold without that exclusion, but not many.

BRK can't sell very much insurance without NCB exclusion.

WTC is the largest workers' compensation event in history—about $1.8 billion in workers' compensation claims. The other day, BRK wrote time-sensitive earthquake insurance—it only pays if the earthquake occurs between 6 am and 6 pm. The Northridge earthquake in 1994 would have been a huge workers' comp event, but it occurred at 4:30 in the morning.

With regard to his prediction about a nuclear attack on a major American city: The chance of anything (NCB) occurring in the next year is very low. Over the next 10 years, that likelihood increases—there are more people in the world, more people hate us, and technology is improving. Over 50 years, that chance increases to a virtual certainty. In the early 1960s, only two countries had nuclear capabilities, and we damn near screwed it up. [He noted there was a good movie on the Cuban missile crisis a couple of years ago. I assume he means "Thirteen Days," which I thought was good.] Now the chances are higher—there are way more people.

4. BRK has a history of striking quick deals and deals done over a handshake. Has there been a change based on the Enron-type financial deceptions?

No. Talked about how he closed the deal with Larson-Juhl, the custom frames maker. Got called up, talked on the phone for 20 minutes, heard the financials and heard the price, flew the guy to Omaha. "I've never seen the company. I hope it's there." [This was actually pretty funny as WEB did an impression of some scam artist: "Hey, what numbers should we report to Warren this month? Ha-ha-ha"] It's a great business—price is not a factor in custom frame purchasing. There are a ton of small framing businesses, dozens in Omaha alone. LJ supplies them all, usually delivering the product within a day. [Is this right? For a custom frame?]

"I could give you $100 million (I'm not going to do that) to build a competing organization. You couldn't do it. It won't double in size, but it's a great business. I can see the durable advantage of that business. You can't mess it up."

We just don't spend a lot of time researching deals. It's like teaching a class on the Efficient Markets Theory. You walk into class on the first day and say, "Everything's priced right." Then what? What else do you need to say? You just don't need that much time. If it's not obvious right away, it won't be obvious with a year's worth of due diligence. (Used Chrysler and Ford as examples.)

Somehow he then moved into a Snickers and Wrigley's example. Snickers has been the top-selling candy bar for 40 years and probably will be in 10 years. If you were chewing spearmint gum 10 years ago, you're still chewing it today. Those are great businesses. If you walked into a store for a Snickers bar and the guy behind the counter offered you a chocolate bar with the same taste and same gooeyness for five cents less, but it was "Joe's Chocolate Bar," you wouldn't buy it. Due diligence—whether or not they have a bad lease or their bad debt reserve is too low, it doesn't matter. It's about the durable advantage.

5. Do you see value in tech stocks today? Is there ever value? Where would BRK invest in tech?

If we could look out five to ten years and see durable advantage and likelihood of high incremental ROE—that would be the place. We're not religious about not investing in tech stocks. ("In fact, I don't even know if there are religions against investing in tech stocks.") "There's no reason to look for a needle in a haystack if the haystack is made out of gold."

You could have bought the pharmaceutical industry in 1993 with a high degree of conviction. Maybe you couldn't identify the one or two winners, but the industry had marvelous economics and you knew there wasn't going to be some new kid on the block to just completely up-end Merck or Schering Plough.

6. Can you speak about investments you made that didn't work out?

Errors tend to be of omission, not commission. Not necessarily Intel or Microsoft, but those situations where he knew the business and did nothing. "Thumb sucking" often happens when he is buying a stock at $x and it goes to $x 1/8. He goes into paralysis. Fannie Mae is one example. Errors of omission have cost BRK billions and billions (20-30 billion).

BRK almost lost a lot on US Airways. "As the ink was drying on the check, they started losing and losing money." Salomon investment; 9/11 insurance—not the fact it was a catastrophe, but that the terrorism insurance wasn't built into the premiums.

The biggest mistake in management is not recognizing that very smart people will do dumb things without trying to. [References Lowenstein book on LTCM] Once an organization starts to gain momentum, it's impossible to stop them. Often happens with acquisitions. If the hurdle rate is 84.3%, the deal will be projected to return 84.4%. If the CEO wants it, it will happen.

7. As you look at the entrepreneurs of the firms you've bought, what do you look for? What advice do you have for potential entrepreneurs?

We look for passion. WEB talked about Al Ueltschi for a while.

Sit down with them and find out if they love the business

or love the money. We've never bought a business from a financial operative. We've never participated in an auction. If a guy auctions his business, we don't want him/it. There's nothing wrong with loving money; it's just not for us.

8. As the best professional in the industry, are you still getting better?

[At this point, Greenwald paraphrases the question as, "Do you still have the mental capacity to do the job?" I'm having flashbacks to Mycroft.]

Investing is great because you're always building a database. Every year you're adding a little bit more (new industries) and there's not that much leakage on the other end. GEICO purchase was a result of his existing database.

"I understand underwear," so Fruit of the Loom wasn't a tough decision.

Everything is cumulative in investing. When he hears something today, it fits in some way into a model built by years of experience.

[Side note: This is an integral part of the whole "no due diligence" phenomenon. They don't necessarily perform due diligence prior to doing a deal precisely because they are performing an abstract version of due diligence on companies and industries every day by adding to their database.]

9. Asbestos payouts seem like they're being accelerated. Comments?

The claims acceleration has tended to be those companies that are in bankruptcy. For companies not in bankruptcy, claims rate hasn't really changed.

BRK has some asbestos claims out there (a lot from Gen

Re) that arose under the normal course of business, and a lot of claims resulting from retro insurance. The deals rely upon timing of payments. BRK is conservative both in the premium demanded and the accounting for the deferred charges. Most asbestos claims are from policies where there is a finite limit.

Overall, payment rate is somewhat slower than anticipated. The results have been perfectly satisfactory so far. [The retro deals, I assume.]

10. What do you see in the underwear business that other people didn't and still don't in Sara Lee (owner of Hanes)? What EBITDA do you see for FoL? What stocks are cheap today?

[I'm cringing at the expected answer to the EBITDA, and I expect a stone wall to the stock tips.]

Basically, EBITDA is worthless.

As far as underwear goes, Hanes and FoL own the market. There are higher-end makes (Calvin Klein, Jockey), but those two control the mass market. Sara Lee (Hanes) pursued an asset-light strategy. [Note: Enron pursued an asset-light strategy—a desire to take assets off balance sheet by removing ownership. Not that I'm really comparing the two.] We control the assets in place at FoL. You can't really buy another version of FoL because if you buy Hanes, you're buying the rest of Sara Lee's portfolio.

Wouldn't be surprised to see FoL earn $130-140 million pre-tax.

Again, we hate EBITDA. Depreciation is the worst kind of expense. (May have even called it despicable.) It's reverse float.

As far as what stocks are cheap, that sounds like a very theoretical question. [Laughs] That's one question I won't answer. Talks about how they keep their activities private.

As far as what companies are in the picture, WEB will never buy a glamorous stock. Money doesn't know where it came from. There's no sense paying more money for a glamorous company if you're getting the same amount of money but paying more for it. It's the same money that you could have gotten from a bland company for a lower cost.

11. General question about the attractiveness of distressed debt.

There's nothing intrinsically good or bad about distressed debt.

FoL was bought at about $0.50 on the dollar. It was a very unusual kind of debt because it kept paying interest during the bankruptcy proceeding, so BRK got a lot of cash from it.

On the Finova transaction: They bought it before it was going to go bankrupt, but knew it was going to. The key there was to evaluate their receivables portfolio (about $14 billion?). WEB estimated a worst-case scenario for the receivables and used that to determine the purchase price.

Comparing the two, Finova hinged on an evaluation of the receivables portfolio; Fruit of the Loom hinged on an evaluation of the brand.

Distressed debt requires more expertise than common stock. There is money to be made on some issues. [At this point, WEB and Schloss start rehashing an old railroad bankruptcy where apparently everyone got rich—Phenomenal level of detail remembered by both of these guys.]

We have never bought a junk bond when it was initially

offered because Wall St. has a special sales push. We buy them later when they get in trouble.

12. What's your take on companies re-incorporating offshore for tax reasons?

I don't like it. I don't like individuals who made the money here living offshore [without paying taxes]. One guy tried to get himself declared an ambassador so he could live in the US full time and still be a foreign citizen. [I think I got that right.] I'd like to think that we (BRK) wouldn't take that opportunity if presented, in the same way I'd like to think I wouldn't walk into a bank and take $1 million if it was just sitting there. But you never know until it happens.

All of the big accounting firms have offered tax strategies, but we're not interested. We have a simple tax return.

On tax rates: Imagine that 24 hours before you're born, you and an effective twin (same DNA, etc.) will be born, one in the U.S. and one in Bangladesh. What percentage of your future income would you pledge to be born in the U.S.? Most likely a pretty high amount. The U.S. offers an extraordinary level of benefits.

13. Pro forma earnings are no good. But how can you look at a company like BRK with a 9/11 event without considering pro forma earnings?

You need to look at the long-term results, but you can't ignore the fact that management missed it (9/11 event). Look at the company's normalized earning power.

Look at this most recent quarter. One of the most benign quarters in insurance, and nothing happened. No "cats" anywhere. You don't see insurance companies reporting good results and saying "Excluding the abnormally low level of claims, we actually would have reported a loss in this quarter."

There are 2 keys to valuing BRK:

- How much cash will the current operating companies be kicking off over the next 10 years?

- What interesting things will be done with that cash in the next 10 years?

[I love it—WEB speaks of real options]

14. On BRK investing abroad:

We'd love to find businesses overseas similar to those we own. We have not had luck to date. Two problems:

- Of the good businesses, most are in the U.S., so there's just not that many abroad.

- BRK is not as well-known overseas, so it's harder for them to get unsolicited calls.

Note that 80% of Coke's earnings are from outside the U.S.

We own 15-20 stocks right now. Three of those are entirely outside of the U.S. We'd be delighted to own any of those three in their entirety at the prices we paid for the piece we do own.

One issue is that reporting requirements are tough. In the U.S, you must disclose upon obtaining 5% of a firm. If you are an insurance company, you must disclose upon obtaining 10% of a firm; if you obtain between 5-10%, you can wait to disclose until year-end. In other countries, that threshold is lower. In the UK, 3% ownership requires disclosure, so our moves are limited.

15. In an investment partnership, how does lack of managerial control (over the firms you invest in) influence decisions?

We have very little influence anyway, even as a director, so it is not a big deal. Very rarely can you change the course as a director and you can't attempt to very often. Someone invited to parties will find he is no longer invited if he is constantly belching at these parties. [Terrible paraphrase… More or less the same quote as he used at the annual meeting two years ago]

Even with 100% owned companies, we accept decisions that we would not have made ourselves. In the long run, they probably balance out to be at least as good as what we would have done. More importantly, it allows the managers to treat the companies as "their" businesses. Do you think Al Ueltschi, who owns $1 billion in BRK stock, is going to want to keep running his business if I'm over his shoulder making decisions?

16. Why don't you sell things when they hit extremely high prices?

We're not selling See's Candy for any amount of money, even if someone offered us 3-4 times its value. Why? It's a quirk of ours. We don't get many opportunities to form associations with good people. When we forge an association, we don't like to ruin it by turning it over to someone else. Small equity pieces are a different matter.

With Buffett Limited Partnership, it was a different matter. It was WEB's job to make the most money possible. Now it's his job to run a business in an agreeable way that hopes to perform well. It's no longer the goal to wring every last dollar out of every situation.

Also talked of the benefits of having a reputation for not selling: [Same masterpiece discussion as recorded elsewhere] When someone builds a business, they're building their own masterpiece. If we purchase that painting, we're offering to hang it, not buy it and quickly sell it to someone else. I tell the prospective seller they can choose to hand it over to BRK, where I will never tell them to add more blue paint or less red paint, but simply hang it. Consider BRK the Metropolitan Museum. Your alternative is to hang it in a porn shop. [I must be delirious. Did he really say this or am I just imagining this whole conversation?]

17. Interest rates are extremely low. What's the lowest benchmark you set?

Good question. I want 13% pre-tax. Over the last couple of years, we made about 8-10 acquisitions, and I think they'll work out to 13% pre-tax. There have been times where the interest rate was 20%, and 13% would be unacceptable. But the opposite doesn't hold. I can't go arbitrarily low with a required return. I'd rather have short-term returns of 1¾% than buy stocks or companies returning 8-9% because I'm going to be holding on to those forever. Those returns are fine now, but enough acquisitions like that and you end up with a very average business.

So in this low-interest environment, we have a lot of money in bonds right now. Either we expect to get more good opportunities or the environment will change.

By the way, the environment will change.

The financial markets have a long history of doing crazy things. You are all young; you'll see those things repeated. [Tells a story about how he has a very old newspaper clipping of a brewer/investor who drowned himself in a vat of hot beer because of troubles arising from excessive margin use] Those things will happen again. You'll have a lot of opportunities to get rich, even if the environment doesn't look like it right now.

18. Describe the H&R Block competitive advantage.

They had a disappointing quarter several years ago, but their franchise was not impaired. The market drove the price down.

Everyone knows H&R. You think of tax preparation, you think of H&R. How many people here can name the number two? Not many. [Apparently Cendant owns it] How much would it take to topple them? The only thing to kill it would be a radical change in the tax laws (e.g., a move to a consumption tax).

We were willing to buy the entire firm at 75% more than what we paid for the piece we bought. [I think he said large insider ownership prevented it, but I'm not sure]

19. (Greenwald: Last question) We moved away from using the first edition of Security Analysis. What are we missing by not using that?

The historical perspective: People will continue to do dumb things.

"History may not repeat itself, but it rhymes." (Twain?)

The first edition is good for a sense of history.

[At this point, he kind of wrapped up.] There are three key things:

1. Margin of safety (Finova deal) is absolutely essential.

2. Look at a stock as a business. "I spent eight years buying stock without thinking of it that way." ["I started at age 11 – I

don't know why I started so late."]

3. Develop the proper attitude towards the market. It is there to serve you, not instruct you. Too many people are instructed by the market.

Student Trek to Meet Warren Buffett
Chairman, Berkshire Hathaway.

May 23, 2005, 10:00 – 11:30 a.m.

The University of Maryland student visit to Omaha to meet with Warren Buffett (WB) on May 23, 2005 began by WB stating that he would answer questions on any subject except University of Nebraska football:

"Last year someone asked the Nebrasda quarterback what the "N" on his helmet stood for. The quarterback responded: "Nowledge."

He then proceeded to respond to 20 questions in the following order…

(1) When do you think the economy in China will slow down?

WB does not expect the economy in China to slow down in a major way in the foreseeable future. The U.S. currently has a $150 billion trade deficit with China, compared to $3 billion in the late 1980s. As a result of the trade deficit, China has been buying U.S. Treasuries. China currently has 1.1 billion people. At the first U.S. Census in 1790, there were 4 million people. At the same time, the population of China was 290 million (almost exactly the same as the U.S. population today). The U.S. has succeeded because our system works. Today the U.S. produces 30% of the world's GDP. China has a population that is as smart as our population, a similar climate, and similar natural resources. Our system is now being adopted by China. Therefore, there is no reason to believe that China cannot be as successful as the U.S.

(2) What is the outlook for GEICO?

A student mentioned that last week six members of our group met with Tony Nicely, the CEO of Berkshire Hathaway owned GEICO. WB then reminisced about his own initial visit to GEICO which also served as his introduction to insurance.

WB was a student in the MBA program at Columbia University. His hero was Professor Benjamin Graham. Since WB had learned that Graham was the Chairman of the Board of GEICO, he decided to visit GEICO (WB was interested in anything that Graham was interested in). He took a train to Washington from New York (1950), arriving on a Saturday morning. Since GEICO's offices were locked, WB banged on the door. When a janitor answered, WB asked if he could meet with "anyone except you." Fortunately, one employee was there – Lorimar Davidson, who spent four hours explaining both insurance and GEICO to WB. WB immediately grasped that GEICO would have an enduring competitive advantage. (Davidson subsequently became CEO of GEICO).

WB was sufficiently impressed that he invested 75% of his net worth of $9,800 in GEICO. When GEICO subsequently got into financial difficulty in the 1970s as a result of bad management (and its stock dropped from 70 to 2 1/8), WB bought about 1/3 of the company for $40 million. His holdings grew to about 50% of the company as a result of stock buybacks by GEICO. In 1996, WB bought the remaining half of the company for $2 billion. GEICO was started by Leo Goodwin and his wife in 1936 with a $200,000 investment.

With respect to automobile insurance, in 1922 State Farm Insurance "had a better idea" by starting a mutual insurance company for personal insurance. They then became the largest insurer. In 1936, GEICO "had a better idea," selling insurance without agents. Today, GEICO has a 6% market share and a $10 billion business. Both Progressive Corporation (with a similar model) and GEICO will be the automobile insurers of the future, and will grow market share over time.

(3) What qualities does WB look for in owners/managers of businesses?

Passion is the most important attribute. The owner or manager must love the business more than money. WB looks for intelligence ("everyone here is smart enough"), business savvy ("some people have it, and some people don't"), energy, and integrity. If someone is lacking in integrity, then WB would prefer someone who is dumb and lazy (can do less damage). The person who lacks integrity can ruin a good business.

(4) How does WB respond to an ineffective manager?

If a manager is not doing his job, then he cannot motivate employees. Occasionally a change needs to be made. Dismissing someone is the only part of his job that he does not like. WB is good at spotting .400 hitters, but he is not good at turning .200 hitters into .400 hitters.

(5) When would WB sell a business?

WB will sell only if the business will permanently lose money, or it has labor problems.

(6) What does WB focus on when reading annual reports?

WB looks for a company with an enduring competitive advantage. He wants to have a good idea of what the economics of the business will look like in 10 years. He seeks a business he understands, one that is within his "circle of competence." If he were a basketball coach, he would look for 7-footers with an enduring advantage, not 5-footers who claim that they have good skills. For WB to make an investment in such a company, the price would also have to be reasonable.

(7) What have been WB's best investments?

WB can follow a company for many years before buying it (if the price declines or there are new factors). He watched Coca-Cola for 30-40 years before buying it in 1988 ("a few factors were being maximized, and the price was right").

Similarly, he followed Gillette for decades, until in 1989 it had the right management and price. Since Berkshire Hathaway owns 8% of Coca-Cola, WB facetiously told the students he did not care whether or not they drank the Coca-Cola products in the conference room, just as long as they "opened the bottle."

WB's best investment was Western Insurance that he discovered in Moody's Manual in 1950. (WB mentioned that he went through all 10,000 pages or so of the manual, which he still keeps in his office.) Western Insurance was earning $20 per share, and the stock price the year before ranged from $3 - $13. He bought at $16, or a price-earnings ratio of less than one, after performing research by interviewing insurance agents and placing newspaper ads to track down some of the 50,000 shares outstanding. Finding Western Insurance in the Moody's Manual, was the equivalent of a "Playboy centerfold with a staple in it" for WB.

(8) What are WB's views on the U.S. trade deficit?

The U.S. is incurring a $2 billion per day current deficit vs. a $12 trillion economy. At this rate, in 10 years we would have to send 3% of our output abroad to pay for this deficit. Although, WB has been shorting the dollar, 80% of his investments are dollar denominated. Recently, when speaking to his friend Bill Gates, WB learned that Gates was also shorting the dollar and making similar currency purchases. WB and Gates looked at each other and said: "We own the money supply of New Zealand." Subsequently, WB and Gates agreed to purchase different currencies.

(9) How do you handle stress?

WB does not have any stress. (He doesn't smoke, doesn't drink, but likes to eat – he "doesn't like to leave any calories behind.")

If we work for someone we admire, there will be no stress. We should avoid stressful situations (the stress isn't worth it). "Taking a job for money is like marrying for money, which is especially dumb if you are already rich." When WB graduated from Columbia, he offered to work for Ben Graham for nothing. Graham said WB "was overpriced." In 1953, when Graham did offer WB a job, WB knew it was the right job.

As a youth, WB enjoyed delivering papers for the Washington Post in part because there was no stress. WB wants to do only what he would do for nothing.

(10) What are WB's views on education, since many of his top managers did not have a college degree?

One can be successful in business if they have desire and energy. Any IQ over 125 is wasted in business or investments. WB visited Wal-Mart last week in Bentonville, Arkansas (Wal-Mart headquarters). At Wal-Mart ordinary people are doing extraordinary things. Susan Jacques is the CEO of Borsheim's Jewelry (a Berkshire Hathaway company). She lacks a college degree, but her leadership has energized her employees. Rose Blumkin (Mrs. B) (started Nebraska Furniture Mart – now a Berkshire Hathaway company) was a Russian émigré who did not speak any English. She learned the language from her 5-year-old daughter who would teach her mother the English words she learned that day in school. Business schools should study Mrs. B. Her business today has revenues of $350 million. Mrs. B could outperform the CEO of any Fortune 500 company. She loved her work so much, that she kept price tags on her furniture at home to remind her of her business. WB discourages his top managers from retiring by telling them that Mrs. B died one year after she retired (at age 103). If you told Mrs. B the dimensions of a room in feet, she could immediately tell you how many square yards of carpet it needs. She even successfully defended herself in court when a competitor sued her for charging prices that were too low. She told the judge that she paid $2 per sq. yd. for a carpet, and sold it for $3.98 per sq. yd. (vs. $5.98 for a competitor). She told the judge that if she raised prices she would be robbing her customers. "How much should I rob my customers?" The judge dismissed the case.

(11) How valuable is a business school education?

WB got a lot out of business school, but it is not a requirement for success in business. He admires professors who inspire their students. Business school students make friends for life among their classmates. If you know who the heroes of young people are, you can predict who will be successful. The earlier someone starts a business (e.g., a lemonade stand, newspaper route, or invests in the stock market), the more successful he/she is likely to be.

(12) What are WB's views on 401(k) plans?

WB recommends 401(k) plans because of matching funds from employers and tax benefits. He recommends buying a low cost index fund on a regular basis to weather the ups and downs (dollar cost averaging), which would also offer tax-free compounding.

"Compounding is amazing – like rolling a snowball down hill, if there is wet snow and a long hill."

(13) What are WB's views on nuclear nonproliferation?

WB believes that this is the number one issue of our time. There are millions of people who are intent on harming others. WB personally and financially supports the Nuclear Threat Initiative (NTI) founded by Ted Turner and Sam Nunn. He also referred to the Einstein-Russell Manifesto. In order to use nuclear weapons, there must be access to knowledge, materials, and deliverability. Knowledge is spreading on the Internet. Our biggest protection comes from the lack of access to materials (nuclear grade plutonium). WB is also concerned about chemical and biological weapons. (e.g., Anthrax could kill as many people as a 10 kiloton bomb in downtown New York.) He is more concerned about governments using these weapons than he is about terrorists.

Some people believe that no government would ever use these weapons, but the U.S. used nuclear weapons in 1945. The world almost had a nuclear World War III in 1962 (Cuban Missile Crisis). We were fortunate that Kennedy and Khrushchev were not influenced by their advisors. If Hitler's anti-Semitism had not chased the best scientists out of his country, Germany may have been the first with nuclear weapons.

(14) What is WB's favorite company owned business?

GEICO is his best investment; it transformed his life. It is his preferred Berkshire company because of its past performance, future potential, and it also is his "oldest child." (He has "40 kids in his family")

(15) What advice do you have for a student who will soon earn an MBA?

"Get on the right train early." "Don't go into the buggy whip business." Last Friday, WB met with Jeff Immelt (CEO of General Electric) and Steve Ballmer (CEO of Microsoft). When they were both 23 years old they shared a cubicle at Procter & Gamble. Soon thereafter they went to their current corporations. (Immelt's father also worked for GE). Take your first job as if it is the last one. Taking jobs as stepping stones to something better is "like saving sex for old age." If you are enthused and fired up about your job it will be found out. "You will jump out from the crowd." Show passion for your work.

(16) What investment advice do you have for students?

Get started investing as soon as possible. WB bought his first stock at age 11. (He wishes he had started sooner.) He bought 3 shares of Cities Service Preferred at $38 ¼. His sister followed him and did the same. The price then declined to $27 and his sister complained every day on the way to school. When the stock recovered to $40, he and his sister sold. WB had a $5 profit. The stock then rose to $200. The lesson WB learned was not to get involved with others on investments, or else their emotions will spill over.

Students should start by actually investing small sums, not just investing on paper. ("There are books on investments and sex. But the real thing is different") Without actually investing, one will not experience the emotions resulting from price increases, as well as price decreases. They should invest in businesses they understand such as McDonald's, Wrigley's, and Coca-Cola. Invest in companies that can be expected to do well in 10 years.

(17) What do you think of real estate?

If money is easy and cheap there will be a lot of speculation. WB just sold a property in Laguna Beach, California. It was sold the first day it was listed for $3½ million ("I made a mistake – I asked too low a price."). His house could be reproduced for $500,000. The land, which therefore sold for $3 million, was 1/20 acre or 2000 sq. feet. Thus, WB sold his land at the rate of $60 million per acre.

There is now a boom in high end real estate. The rich have never been richer ("in part as a result of our tax system.") The boom feeds on itself. In 1980 WB bought a nearby farm for $600 per acre. In the mid-1980s, banks were lending at a 10% interest rate for the purchase of farms at a price of $2,000 per acre. Banks then failed all over the state. People were buying farms for "asset appreciation" and paid no attention to income from the farm. The farms could produce income of $80 per acre, but the financing cost was $200 per acre (10% interest on $2,000 per acre price.) Therefore, those who purchased at $2000 per acre were *losing* $120 ($200 - $80) per acre. (Note: At WB's purchase price of $600 per acre, and assuming 10% financing, the financing cost would be $60 per acre – resulting in a *profit* of $20 ($80 - $60) per acre.)

One characteristic of bubbles is that people buy assets only for price appreciation and ignore income considerations. Lots of money can be made in the aftermath of bubbles. One example was the opportunity to have bought assets from the Resolution Trust Corporation in the early 1990s. Market bubbles will happen again.

Prices may be declining now in high priced real estate. When "the lenders are gone" and the "sellers sell," prices decline.

(18) Do hedge funds pose a risk to the overall economy?

Unless the hedge funds are highly leveraged and are all on one side, they do not necessarily have to have a system wide impact. Institutions today are looking for the Holy Grail. Hedge funds have grown rapidly with $1 trillion invested in them. WB is willing to place a large bet that the 10 largest hedge funds today will not outperform the

S&P 500 over the next ten years. (This was not the case 30 years ago when there were few hedge funds with few dollars invested in them.) In the fall of 1998, Long Term Capital Management (LTCM) failed when they were buying the 29½ year U.S. Treasury bond with a 10 basis point difference in yield versus the 30 year bond. LTCM bet the difference would narrow over time. (But it subsequently widened to 30 basis points.) LTCM simultaneously sold short the very liquid 10 year Treasury note. However, when there was a financial panic, there was a stampede into the 10 year Treasury note. LTCM was then forced to unwind its positions.

(19) Is outsourcing a problem?

Outsourcing is not the problem. Trade is good. The trade deficit is the problem.

(20) What is more important, the right people or the right business?

If you put the right people in the wrong business, the bad

economics of the business will prevail. On the other hand, the wrong people will ruin a good business. What you need are the right people in the right business. ("Then you can let the snowball roll.")

Lunch at Gorat's

(12:00 – 1:30 p.m.)

– WB joined the group for lunch at his favorite restaurant, Gorat's. He drove four students to the restaurant. His license plate: "THRIFTY."

– WB's favorite book is Katharine Graham's autobiography, "Personal History."

– WB hates meetings and has never had one at Berkshire Hathaway.

– WB has never sold a share of Berkshire Hathaway stock, although he has given away some of his shares.

– A student asked whether a company like Google has an enduring competitive advantage. WB said that GEICO recently sued Google over keyword advertising programs and trademark infringement. So far, Google has been winning the legal battle. Brin and Page are very smart individuals. However, WB said that his friend Bill Gates (Microsoft) wants to "kill" them. In 10 years, very few tech/Internet firms will be in the top 25 by sales, even though they will have had a big impact on our lives.

– WB mentioned that 10 years from now Wal-Mart will be the largest retailer in the world, and one of the top five companies in the world in terms of sales. Exxon Mobil might possibly be in the top five as well.

– What to look for in a wife/spouse?

Warren Buffett Chairman, Berkshire Hathaway

It's a tremendously important decision. Look for someone who will love you unconditionally and will subtly encourage you to be better than you thought you can be.

WB told the story of a man who spent 20 years looking for the perfect woman. When he finally found her, she unfortunately was looking for the perfect man.

– What good is money?

It buys time and flexibility to do what you want (work how you want). But it doesn't really make a huge difference in other things. WB does not want more money to enhance his obituary. WB sleeps for 7 hours a day on a mattress like everyone else. He enjoys playing bridge online as much as doing much more expensive things (e.g., spending time with friends on a yacht).

– You can buy sex, but you can't buy love. The only way to get love is to be lovable.

– A person is rich if they have many friendships. WB knows a woman who survived a concentration camp but was slow to make friends because she wondered if they would hide her. WB says that a person is rich if they know many people who would hide them.

– WB mentioned that all the students are invited back to Omaha for Berkshire Hathaway's next annual meeting (May 2006). They do not have to be shareholders to attend. If the students just mention his name, "they may let you in."

– WB treated the students to lunch.

– WB then posed for several group pictures.

Warren Bufet Talks Business.

Peter Lynch has always said: "Buy a business that's so good that any idiot could run it because sooner or later one will." Well, all I know is if I buy the right kind of business at the right price with the right people, I'll do well over time.

I really had a lesson on unemployment a few years ago. On August 14th of 1991 I got a phone call at a quarter of seven in the morning. It was the top management of Solomon, and they told me at a quarter of seven essentially that the head of the Fed of New York – who was the most powerful man in finance, basically – told them that the top management was unacceptable and that therefore they were going to offer their resignations and there was no one there to run the place. And that was a matter of some concern because at the time Solomon had balance-sheet totals of 150 billion dollars, of which about 4 billion was equity and the other 146 billion was owed to someone else. And that was the largest amount owned by any American corporation except for City Corps at that time. It was larger than the liabilities of the Prudential Insurance Company, larger than the liabilities of the Bank of America, Merrill Lynch, American Express – whatever. And there was one problem about this 146 billion that a very high percentage of it came due within a few weeks.

And so that was the situation, and I went back to New York that day, on that Friday, and I met that evening – and this is where it may start getting relevant to this group – one of the problems I was going to have the following week was I needed somebody to run the place. There were 8,000 people and this 150 billion of balance-sheet assets and liabilities and a complex business. And essentially, somebody had to be making decisions minute-by-minute about the operations because I was going to have to be dealing with regulators and legislators and people of that sort.

So I met twelve people, roughly twelve, that evening – a dozen or so, and I probably knew four or five of them by sight; and there were probably six or seven that I didn't know or I probably knew their names. So as I interviewed these people, making what for me was the most important hire by far that I ever had to make, it may be of interest to you because it may not be quite as dramatic a time when you get hired, but there may be some of the same things going through the mind of the person looking at you.

The good news is I did not ask them their grades in business school. And the bad news, of course, is I didn't ask them if they had been to business school at all. I never looked at a resume. It wouldn't have made any difference. I knew that all twelve had the IQ to handle the job. No one had gotten to that position in the firm without being smart enough to know all the instruments and to know how markets work and all of that sort of thing. So it wasn't a question of IQ at all. It's just sort of hearing how their machinery works. You can tell the people that are very full of themselves – that's very easy to do. You find a few of those in investment banking, believe it or not. And you know, you can probably detect perhaps that ones that aren't going to have the courage in a situation like that.

But I wanted the qualities – you know, the same thing Ben Franklin wrote about a couple hundred years ago: The people who are always willing to give the other person more credit than themselves and who don't cut corners and who deliver all they promise and a little extra. And essentially, I was very lucky because I found an individual – a fellow named Derek. The next day the board met and we had all the complications that day, and we had a group of about 200 reporters, probably about this size, in an auditorium who had come in on Sunday to cover the story. And I walked out of the director's meeting about a quarter of three – it was late because of other problems. And there were these twelve boys, and I just walked up to Derek and I tapped him on the chest and I said: "You're it, pal." And we went right down to the auditorium and 200 or so reporters fired questions at him for three hours while he sat up at the podium with about two minutes' notice that he was going to be running the firm.

A month later, Derek remembered to ask me what he was getting paid. The question of his salary had never come up. Forget about stock options or anything like that – never came up. He just walked right up and never said a word about it and took on the job, worked 18-hour days for months and months and months, showed uncanny judgment about what to bring up to me and what not to bring up to me, and all sorts of things like that.

And I often use this illustration with a class. I say to them: If you looked under your seat today and one of you won this lucky ticket, and the one who got that ticket got to pick one of their classmates – you'd been together for a couple of years or whatever – and you get to pick one of your classmates, and you could pick anyone you wanted to and you had an hour to make the decision, and you would get 10% of the earnings of that individual for the rest of their life – you don't pick the guy with the richest father in the class. But what would you think about in that hour in terms of who you picked? Would you think about who had the highest grades in the class? Probably not. Would you think about who had the highest IQ? Probably not. The best-looking? Probably not. A whole bunch of things would go through your mind. I think you'd be amazed at how most of you would settle on a relatively few individuals.

But the interesting thing is that when you think about what's going through your mind, you're not thinking about things that are impossible for you to achieve yourself. You're not thinking about who can jump seven feet, who can throw a football 65 yards, who can recite Pi at 300 digits or whatever it may be. You're thinking about a whole bunch of qualities of character. And the truth is that every one of those qualities is obtainable. They're largely a matter of habit. My old boss, Ben Graham, when he was 12 years old, wrote down all the qualities that he admired in other people, and he wrote down the qualities that he found objectionable. And he looked at this list and there wasn't anything there about being able to run the 100-yard dash in 9.6 or high-jumping seven feet. They were all things that were simply a matter of deciding whether you were going to be that kind of person or not.

And when you're young, you really have that opportunity, whereas when you get older it gets tougher because somebody has said: "The chains of habit are too light to be felt until they're too heavy to be broken." And in terms of behavior, I see that all the time. So the time to form the right habits is very early, but the right habits – the habits that you will admire in someone else and want to buy 10% of whatever the individual earns – they're absolutely obtainable. And if you had to sell short one other member of your class – you know, these deals always come with a hooker – and you had to pay 10% of their earnings – again, you wouldn't pick the person with the lowest grades or anything. You would think about the person who always cut corners or claimed credit for things that they didn't do, never showed up on time – all these little things that seem like nothing, but they determine whether if you have a 300-horsepower motor whether you get 300-horsepower output on it or whether you get a whole lot less. And the people I see that function well are not necessarily the people with the biggest motors but they're the people with the most efficient motors. And it's those qualities of character that really make an enormous difference.

So what I would suggest to you is think about that person you'd buy 10% of, and the one you'd short 10% of, and think about why you would do it. And then ask yourself: What on this left-hand side of the list can I achieve myself and what on the right-hand side of the list can I get rid of myself if I possess it? And in the end, decide you're going to be the person that you'd buy the 10% of.

That's enough of the sermon. I'd like to answer questions

now. And really, the nastier they are the better I like it because it's much more fun. It makes it more interesting. So let's start off with one here.

QUESTION: Mr. Buffet, I was reading – it sounds like your and Charlie Munger's analysis of some companies is very back-of-the-envelope. Could you just tell us about the financial analysis that you do on companies, whether it be Rose Blumkin's Furniture Mart or whether it be Coca Cola?

MR. BUFFET: Well, those are two good examples – the furniture mart in Omaha that's going to do at one location $230 million of business. It's more than twice as much business as any other furniture or single-store furniture operation in the country. It's not really run by her now, but she is still the spiritual head of the place – a woman named Rose Blumkin is going to be 101 years of age in December, and she came over here and landed in Seattle with a tag around her neck and couldn't speak a word of English. The Red Cross got her to Iowa first, and then she came over and started this store after bringing over her seven siblings and her mother and father from Russia. She started this store with $500, and now has a store that does $230 million. She works seven days a week. She's working as we talk – she'll be working Sunday – an amazing woman.

And the punch line – she put all these people out of business – is that she can't read or write. You know, her business will make $22 million or $23 million pre-tax this year. If you told her this room was 47 x 38, she would tell you how many square yards that is in her head and extend it out at $5.98 a yard and add the sales tax and knock off something because she liked you. It is a real story. So I would say, incidentally, on something like that – that's all the analysis you need. If you can buy into a business that's run by somebody...or with her family, that runs it that way... Our total legal and accounting fees in buying that business were $1,400, and it was a one-page contract that just affirmed that she owned the place and that I was going to get good title. There was no audit. I never looked to see what the real estate records were on the 60 acres or anything of the sort, but I just knew that anything she said was so. And you feel very comfortable buying a business like that.

I think any good investment idea probably could be put in one paragraph. Now there are all kinds of investment ideas that I'm not going to be able to understand. I believe very strongly, as does Mrs. B. – as Rose Blumkin is called – I believe very strongly in operating with what I call "my circle of competence." And the most important thing in terms of your circle of competence is not how large the area of it is; it's how well you define the perimeter. If you know where the edges are, you're way better off than somebody that's got one that's five times as large but they get very fuzzy around the edges. And I could understand some kinds of simple businesses; I can't understand complicated businesses.

Coca Cola is about 110 years old now and selling 750 million eight-oz. servings of their products a day around the world; per capita consumption going up in virtually every country in the world after about 110 years or so. It has 47% of the soft drink consumption throughout the world outside the United States, 41 % in the United States and gaining share every year. It isn't very complicated. You have to decide, A, whether it's a product that is somewhat durable, which I think has been illustrated; and whether the appeal is universal, which it certainly is, and then whether you have honest and competent management running it, which you most certainly do.

Peter Lynch has always said: "Buy a business that's so good that any idiot can run it because sooner or later one will." Well, we would like to buy a business like that and then we would like a terrific guy running it, and we had two terrific people at Coke running it. All we're trying to do is try and find businesses we think we can understand where we like the people running them and where the place makes sense in relation to the future economics. And when I find that, I like to buy a lot of it and keep it. And they're hard enough to find that I don't believe in selling them very often because it's hard to find replacements.

QUESTION: Mr. Buffet, how do you know when to sell a business? When is the time to do that?

MR. BUFFET: Well, the question about selling a really great business is never. Because to sell off something that is a really wonderful business because the price looks a little high or something like that is almost always a mistake. It took me a long time to learn that and I haven't fully learned it yet, but it's rare that it makes sense. If you really believe that the long-term economics of the business are terrific, it's very rare it makes any sense to sell it.

Now if you get into some technology company or something where five guys are out in a garage some place doing something that's going to change the whole industry, that's beyond me anyway. And if you try to jump from flower to flower among groups like that I think you'd probably have to because I'm not sure that you can pick permanent winners.

But I would say that if you keep it very simple – we own a lot of Gillette, for example. There are 21 billion razor blades used in the world a year. Thirty percent of those are Gillette's, but 60% by value are Gillette's. They have 90% market shares in some countries – in Scandinavia and in Mexico. Now when something has been around as long as shaving and you find a company that has that kind of both innovative power in terms of developing better razors all the time, plus the distribution power and the position in people's minds – you know, for an item that only costs 20 bucks a year… Here's something that you do every day and for 20 bucks a year you get a terrific shaving experience – now men are not inclined to shift around a lot when they get that kind of a situation. I like businesses where I think I know what it's going to look like in 5, 10, 15 or 20 years. I think I know what Gillette will look like, and I think I know what Coke will look like.

For one thing, you go to bed feeling very comfortable just thinking of 2.5 billion males with hair growing while you sleep… No one at Gillette has trouble sleeping! It's like investments – that's the beauty of the investment business. I don't have to be right on all of these companies I don't understand. I don't have to be right on Oracle Systems or Microsoft or DuPont; I just have to be right on one decision a year. It's a beautiful business that way.

You know, I was in the department store business for a while – don't ask me why. But I was in it, and if my competitor had air-conditioning, I had air-conditioning. If my competitor offered 18-month terms instead of 12-month terms, I had to offer it. If he put in an escalator, I had to put in one. All of those were defensive decisions. I had to make those like that – he was throwing pitches at me and I had to swing, no matter whether the ball was good or not. But in investments, there is no such thing as a called strike. You can stand there at the plate and the pitcher can throw a ball right down the middle. If it's General Motors at 47 and you don't know enough to decide on General Motors at 47, you let it go right on by, and no one's going to call a strike. The only way you can have a strike is to swing and miss. And therefore, you can look at hundreds and thousands of pitches – thousands of companies on the New York Stock Exchange.

Every single day companies are trading and every day they trade at different prices, and all you have to do is look for the few that you can understand and then wait until somebody offers you a selling price, if you're on the buy side. And it happens often enough that it gets quite interesting, but it doesn't happen all the time, and if you try to make it happen too often you get in trouble.

I've often said that if you're at business school and if you've got a punch card with 20 punches on it when you left school, and every time you made an investment decision that you used up one punch, you'd get very rich because you would think about every single one you made, and when you knew enough to make a decision, you'd do it on a big scale. Buying businesses on Wall Street is so easy. You can buy one at 10 o'clock and sell it 10:05, and you know, you can become a part owner of General Electric at 10:10. But the very ease with which that can be done causes people to do a lot of things that don't make a lot of sense. But most of the fortunes have been made in relatively few securities, and ones that were held for a very long time, and ones that the buyer understood.

QUESTION: Mr. Buffet, you invest in companies with managers that you say you like and you trust and admire, and I'd like to know who you like and trust and admire in politics and business today.

MR. BUFFET: Well, in business I can tell you there's nobody that I admire more than the CEO of Cap Cities, Tom Murphy. I admire Roberto Goizueta and Don Keough who retired recently, but they were one of the great two-manager combinations in the history of business at Coke. They took the market value from $5 billion to now $60 billion in a matter of eleven or twelve years. Tom Murphy worked with Dan Burke – a tremendous combination. It's a business I don't know anything about. I admire Bill Gates enormously. I know him individually and I think he's incredible in business.

I only believe in working with people I like. I mean, we have a very small office; we have maybe ten or eleven people there. But I think it's crazy to take a job or work with people who cause your stomach to churn and keep you up at night and all of that. If you're in a job like that, think about changing it. Working with people you don't like in business is really like marrying for money, which is probably a bad idea under any circumstances, but it's crazy if you're already rich, right? So I work with people I like. I tap dance every day to work, and I'm with people that I think are terrific. I admire them.

Some student at Harvard asked me at a talk last year: "Who should I go to work for?" I said: "Well, go to work for whomever you admire the most." I got a call from the dean about two weeks later, and he said: "What did you tell these kids? They're all becoming self-employed."

QUESTION: Mr. Buffet, I would like to buy a share of Berkshire-Hathaway, but unfortunately my cash flow is a little tight now. Have you considered splitting the stock?

MR. BUFFET: Yeah, I get asked that occasionally. I've got a philosophy about shareholders. Essentially, if you're a public company, anybody can become your partner in the business. If I was going to decide to build a motel here or start a mini-steel company, I could invite ten or twelve people to be my partners and I would be sure they would be compatible with me because I'd select them and they'd select me.

In a private business, a private partnership, you should get a good relationship among the owners because they have a chance to sit down and decide who wants to be associated with whom. But in a public company anybody can buy in. You could have anybody – the only qualification is money, which as you mentioned sometimes is a limiting factor.

But at Berkshire I want to get people as shareholders, as partners of mine, who have the same expectations, the same time horizons, the same methods of measurement that I have. I mean, it's crazy to go into business with somebody who's got entirely different expectations than you have. So the only way I can affect that – since anybody can buy it – is by my communications and policies. I will try to follow policies and I will try to communicate with the people who are my partners or my would-be partners so that the right kind of people in terms of expectations – I don't mean the right kind of people that are the sort of people you want to have at a cocktail party or something – but the people who are going to be happy when I'm happy with results, and who are going to be unhappy when I'm unhappy.

The worst thing in the world, though – we could stick a sign outside this hall tonight and we could put "rock concert" on it and we'd have one kind of crowd come in. And we could put "valet" and we'd have a somewhat different kind of crowd come in. Both crowds are fine, but it's a terrible mistake to put "rock concert" out there if you're going to have a valet or vice versa. And the only way I have of sticking a sign on Berkshire as to the kind of place I'm asking people to enter is through the communications and policies.

Splitting the stock is a relatively minor item in that. But essentially, I would rather have people as owners that A, expect to own it the rest of their lives. Ideally, I don't want anybody that's going to think about selling it next week or next month or next year. They may change their mind and that's fine, but I really want them to go in with the idea that they're going into a partnership with me for the rest of their lives. And if they're buying because they think the stock is going to be split for a while or because they thing the earnings are going to be up next quarter or something like that, they're not terrible people, but they are going to change their mind after they get in the hall and they're going to think this is the wrong kind of place.

All the seats are going to be occupied. That's the nature of the stock market. All of the shares of General Motors or Berkshire-Hathaway or General Electric are going to be owned by somebody. It makes sense, in my view, to follow policies that get people that are as close to you in objectives and expectations that you can have. And by not splitting we have eliminated some people we wouldn't like to eliminate, but we've also eliminated all of the bad people that are basically interested in trading stocks actively. And that's a good group, from my standpoint.

The New York Stock Exchange is not wild about it because we have by far the lowest turnover relative capitalization of any stock on the Exchange. But that to me is terrific. If I had a club or if I was preaching in a church, I would not measure my success by how frequent the turnover of the congregation was or the club membership. I would really like the idea that nobody wanted to leave their seats so there wasn't any seat available for someone else.

QUESTION: I was wondering if you could share a story with us as one of your investment non-successes or failures, and maybe why it failed and maybe some of the lessons you learned from that failure that would be helpful to us.

MR. BUFFET: I make more mistakes when I have a lot of cash around. I think my decision-making acuity folds or fades with extra cash because I just think there's just more of a compulsion to do something when you're sitting around with cash than if you have to either sell something or maybe borrow money, although we're not big on borrowed money. So I would say that that's been one causal factor over the years. Fortunately, most of the time I haven't had much cash around so that hasn't been a major problem, but it has caused me – I like to think that's what caused it; maybe it was just plain stupidity at the time.

It's interesting: I made a study back when I ran a partnership of all our larger investments versus the smaller investments. The larger investments always did better than the smaller investments. There is a threshold of examination and criticism and knowledge that has to be overcome or reached in making a big decision that you can get sloppy about on small decisions. You know, somebody says, I bought 100 shares of this or that because I heard about it at a party the other night. Well, there is that tendency with small decisions to think you can do it for not very good reasons. So I think larger decisions are helpful in that regard.

We have generally not had large losses relative to capital. The largest loss we've ever had, even in the partnership from Berkshire, probably was 2% of net worth. So the nature of not doing very many things and being careful about them probably will keep you from making big errors of commission.

Now errors of omission are the ones that are the big sins. I wrote in a report a couple of years ago – I've got a thing in my report called "Mistake De Jour" and I manage to come up with one every year too. And I started out to buy Fanny Mae, for example, back in 1988 or so, and for one reason or the other I just didn't follow through. We could have made about a billion and a half dollars on that! I think we made about 5 million. Those are the mistakes you don't see. The mistakes you don't see, in our case, are way bigger than the mistakes that you see.

We owned 5% of the Walt Disney Company in 1966. The whole Walt Disney Company was selling for $80 million in 1966 debt-free – $4 million was 5% of the company. They spent $17 million on the Pirate's Ride in 1966. Here was a company selling at less than five times the rides, and they had a lot of rides! I mean, that is cheap. I remember that the knock-out on Wall Street that was earning a lot of money that year was "Mary Poppins," and there wasn't anything coming next year. And I remember I went to see "Mary Poppins" at a theater on Broadway, about 45th, at about two in the afternoon. I had a little attaché case and I'm going to see "Mary Poppins." I got up to this woman at the ticket booth and I said: "I've got a kid around here some place, you know. I'm taking him."

Here they were: They had two hundred and some films of one sort or the other in the can at that point. They had 300 acres down at Anaheim with Disneyland growing at that time – nine million people a year – and the whole place was selling for 80 million bucks. So we bought 5% for $4 million, and the great news is we sold 5% for $6 million about a year later. That 5% now would be worth about a billion. But you don't see that. Conventional accounting doesn't pick that up, but that's the kind of mistake I've made.

QUESTION: Mr. Buffet, what prompted you to make an investment in US Air given the fact that this is such a cut-throat industry and certainly not transparent and easily understandable?

MR. BUFFET: Well, I think that probably the best answer is temporary insanity. The fellow who runs US Air is a wonderful guy. He just happens to be in an extraordinarily tough business. And the interesting thing is I had actually written something for Graham's book in the early '70s about how the airline business was about the toughest business there was. And the interesting thing, of course, is that if you go back to the time of Kitty Hawk – the airline transport business in the United States – net has made no money. I mean, just think if you'd been down there at Kitty Hawk and you'd seen this guy go up, and all of the sudden this vision hits you that tens of millions of people will be doing this all over the world someday and it would bring us all closer together. And then you'd think: My God, this is something to be in on. And then despite putting in billions and billions and billions of dollars, the net return for owners – if you owned it all and you'd put up all this money – is less than zero. If there had been a capitalist down there, the guy should have shot down Wilbur. You know, one small step for mankind and one huge step backwards for capitalism, but anyway…

So along comes 1989 and I've got a lot of cash, and no one misled me in any way, shape or form. I mean, this is entirely 100% my decision, and I put money in it. And you can't find a better human being or manager than mine, but he is operating with revenues based on market factors and costs that are not based on market factors, and that's a recipe for a lot of trouble. So I now have this 800-number, and if I ever get the urge to buy an airline stock, I dial this number and I say: My name is Warren and I'm an air-a-holic, and then this guy talks me down on the other end.

I never think about what the stock market is going to do because if Walt Disney had come to me in 1966, and it was a private company, and he said: Would you like to buy 5% of this company for $4 million? I would not think about what the stock market was going to do. I would think about what I thought the Walt Disney Company was going to do over time. And if in 1988 **Roberto** Goizueta – let's say Coca Cola had been private – and he had come to me and said: Do you want to buy six-and-a-fraction percent of the Coca Cola Company for a billion dollars? I would look at the Coca Cola Company. So if something occurs to me to be intelligent to do, I'm not going to forego doing it because I or anybody else has an opinion about the stock market.

If Alan Greenspan came up and whispered in my ear and said: I think bonds are going to do this or that, and therefore stocks... I wouldn't pay any attention – not because I don't respect Alan Greenspan; it's just I'm not going to trade something I know how to do and give up something I know how to do because of some opinion about something I don't know how to do. And I don't know how to predict the stock market; I don't know how to predict interest rates; I don't know how to predict business. All I know is if I buy the right kind of business at the right price with the right people, I'll do well over time.

And in stocks, it's very hard to know when something will happen, and it's very easy to know what will happen. We bought See's Candy in 1972. That wouldn't be very familiar too much on the East Coast but it's very dominant in boxed chocolates on the West Coast. It so happened that the founder wanted to sell the company. Now I wouldn't think about what the stock market's going to do when I go and decide whether to buy See's Chocolates. What I'm thinking about is whether Russell Stover can knock them out of the box or you can raise your prices periodically as you go along, how strong their hold is on people who are chocolate consumers in the West. And if that's my attitude toward buying 100% of a business like See's, it's also going to be my attitude toward buying six percent of a business like Coca Cola. In other words, why in the world should I pass up the chance?

Coca Cola went public in either 1919 or 1920 at $40 a share. The Kantor family had sold it through – I guess it would have been then J.P. Morgan, the predecessor company, and the trust company Georgia, which is now a part of SunTrust. The fee was two hundred-and-some thousand dollars for this $25 million-dollar offering, and Morgan took theirs in cash; the trust company of Georgia took theirs in stock. So you'll see on the trust company at Georgia or SunTrust balance sheet a little item "investment in Coca Cola" with a cost of $110,000. It's worth a little over a billion dollars now.

And subsequent to going public, the stock went down over 50%. That's when Mr. Woodruff came back from Cleveland where he was working with the White Motor Company and they brought him back to run it. They had a problem with the bottlers because of some contractual arrangements. They had made a bad deal back in 1989 in terms of the original bottling contract, and sugar prices had shot up after World War I and there were various problems.

Now let's say that back in 1919 you had seen that we would have the Great Depression, when the country's social fabric was really strained as to whether the country would even hold together. You'd have World War II. You'd have nuclear weapons. You'd have – a million things could happen. Any one of those you could say: Well, if that's going to happen maybe I'd better wait a little while before I buy Coke. But the answer was that if you bought the Coke stock one share for $40 dollars at the start of the year, or $19 at the end of the year, and you reinvested dividends, you'd have about 2.5 million dollars now for each share. And it's so important to be in the right businesses. It would be wonderful if you could pick out the right time as well – you know, just the time to buy it. But I don't feel I can do that.

So I don't care, really, whether the Dow is at 3900 or what the outlook will be for businesses because I'm not going to sell See's Candy. I'm not going to sell the Buffalo News. I'm not going to sell H.H. Brown, the shoe company which has a first-class operation here at Carolina Shoe. I'm not going to sell those businesses because the market was high or something of the sort. I want to own good businesses, and if it doesn't make sense to sell those...Why should I sell the shares of Gillette I've got, because I look at those as parts of businesses. I have no idea if I come back here in two years whether the stock market will be higher or lower. I do know all of the intelligent things to do between now and then, and that if you see one, the thing to do is to do it.

QUESTION: From your point of view, what's the difference in investing in the entire company like See's versus just a piece of a company like Coca Cola?

MR. BUFFET: Well, there's way less difference than most people think, in my view. If I own all of See's at Berkshire and we want to change the management, we can change the management. But I don't want to get into managements we need to change in the first place. I mean, if I were going to buy See's and I thought I needed to change the management, I might not buy it because what do I know about making chocolates? So I want to find them with good management. But it is true that if you had a managerial problem and you owned it all, you could change it.

It is also true that you could take the capital – the earnings out of a business that you control 100% of. You can decide the distribution policy and them over some place else, and that's an advantage to us. If the XYZ Company that we own 5% of wants to go out and buy movie studios or whatever they might want to do, they get to allocate the capital; and all things being equal or even unequal I would rather allocate the capital, and I could do that if we own 100%. So that's the advantage of owning 100%.

But it's so much more important to own a good business and to be in with good managers than to have this little extra advantage of being able to change managers. I would rather own a good business than to own all of it. I mean, I'd like to own all of Coca Cola, but I'm not going to own all of Coca Cola. So is that a reason not to buy 7%? No. So the one advantage we have at Berkshire is that we have this mental flexibility where all we're doing is trying to figure out how to put the capital into good businesses. And we're not in the steel business per se; we're not in the shoe business per se; we're not in any business per se. We're big in insurance, but we're not committed to it. We don't have a mindset that says you have to go down this road. So we can take capital and we can move it into businesses that make sense, and that is an advantage. And since I don't come up the route from any one of these businesses, I've got that advantage of being somewhat detached, perhaps, and therefore objective. And then the question is whether it's smart, but at least I should be objective about it.

Banking consolidation: Well, it's going to continue in a big way. Most managers like to grow, and they like to grow intelligently if they can, but if they can't, they're also willing to grow in other ways. And you know, every year the American Banker – which is the daily banking publication – every year they list what used to be thirteen or fourteen thousand banks by size. They don't list them by profitability. And the first one hundred, they used to show the pictures of the CEOs of the 100 largest banks. And I think that that probably has some effect. If you start measuring yourself by size – they measure by assets, but the assets are always balanced off by liabilities in that strange accounting convention. It's the only business in the world where people brag about how much they owe – you know, they say, I got a hundred-billion-dollar bank, which means I owe a hundred billion or close to it.

But I myself do not see, among the banks I look at, economies of scale beyond certain points. There's always an advantage in being dominant in a market, but I'm not sure whether if you've got $200 billion spread across the country and 15% market shares, you're going to have a better business than the guy who's got 30% of the market in Rockford, Illinois.

We used to own a bank in Rockford, Illinois, which made 2% on assets after tax and was conservative in every respect. But that bank would earn less money as part of a larger institution. I'm convinced of that. So I don't see great advantages to shareholders in terms of major expansions of banks. I'm not saying it's all a mistake because I've seen some good acquisitions – Wells Fargo made a terrific acquisition of Crocker, for example, some years back. But I think it will continue, and I think public bank shareholders are going to be a little luckier than the acquiring bank shareholders.

QUESTION: I was wondering if you could comment on your perspective of investments outside of the U.S., and in particular address your perspective on how you would hedge currency risk.

MR. BUFFET: Gillette makes about two-thirds of its money outside of the United States, and we own about 11% of Gillette. And Coke makes over 80% of its money outside the United States, and we own 7.7% of Coke. We love the kind of companies that can do well on international markets, obviously, and particularly where they're largely untapped. Would we buy Coca Cola if instead of being domiciled in Atlanta, it was domiciled in London or Amsterdam or some place? The answer, of course, is yes. Would I like it quite as well? Probably just a tiny notch less because there might be nuances of corporate governance factors or tax factors or attitudes toward capitalists or anything else that I might not understand quite as well, even in England, as I might in the United States.

So I prefer – by a small margin to many countries and by a large margin to other countries – I prefer a U.S. domicile operation. But I also prefer businesses that earn high returns on capital and all of that sort of thing, so we will look any place to find a good business. I find it easier to find them in the U.S. I understand the accounting a little bit better and I just probably have more insight into how they're going to function in the future, a little more here than in some other country. But I don't rule them out.

On the other hand, the U.S. equity market is a five trillion-dollar market, and if I can't make money in a five-trillion-dollar market, it may be a little bit of wishful thinking to think all I have to do is get a few thousand miles away and I'll start showing my stuff...

QUESTION: You and Mr. Munger have long talked about franchise value of businesses. And without tipping your hat, I'm just curious as to what areas you perceive that have franchise value right now?

MR. BUFFET: Well, the real test of franchise value is if they don't have your product, but they have something that somebody else says is similar, does the would-be purchaser walk out of the store or walk across the street and buy it? So if you go in and you say: I'd like a Hershey bar, and they say: We don't have Hershey bars but we have this unmarked chocolate bar that the owner of the place recommends. If you walk across the street to buy a Hershey bar, or if you'll pay a nickel more for the bar than the unmarked bar or something like that, that's franchise value. And you have to maintain that in people's minds.

That was our concern. When we bought See's Candy, candy was selling for $1.95 a pound. The question was would people pay more for that candy as the years went along and inflation took place? And the truth is that if people perceive that it's the best candy, or a significant percentage of them do in the area, or the dominant percentage do, you're going to do very well with a business like that. The franchise is in their mind. It's the experience they had – I mean, it's the first time they handed it to a girl and she kissed him afterwards, or whatever, or slapped him. I mean, that's what we like them to do with the competitor's candy. And you know they're not going to go home on Valentine's Day and say: Here, honey, here's two pounds of chocolate, I took the low bid. It just doesn't work!

So if you've got the right kind of product that way, if you're Wrigley's chewing gum or whatever it may be – you may be paying for taste in this case; you may be paying for a mental association you have for something; you may be paying for service available or a lot of things. That's franchise value.

And then the question is how durable is it? How big is it and how durable is it? And I say that franchise is basically like a moat around your economic castle. Now there are two things that are important: How big is the castle? Coco Cola is a big castle. See's Candy is not a very big castle, but it's a castle. And around both of those there's a moat, and that moat is either slightly eroding or slightly growing all the time. It may be based on advertising, it may be based on service, it may be based on employee training, it may be based on research – a lot of things. There are all kinds of things you're trying to do to make that moat bigger and bigger and to throw more piranha and crocodiles, etc., into the moat. And you need a moat in business to protect you from some guy who is going to come along and offer it for a penny cheaper. That's what we're looking for all the time. And you know, you're not going to find it in carbon steel; you're not going to find it with an integrated oil company or something of the sort, in all likelihood.

But you will find it – you don't have to find very many – only very few. If you have ten good ideas in the rest of your life, you can afford to give away five of them because you'll get very rich with a very few good ideas. If you understand an idea, you can express it so other people understand it. It's interesting – I find that every year when I write the report. I hit these blocks, and the block isn't because I've run out of words in the dictionary; the block is because I haven't got it straight in my own mind yet. And there's nothing like writing to force you to think and get your thoughts straight. If you want to communicate something to other investors or co-owners or whatever it may be, it's quite possible to do it. And I think based on what Sherman Lovett said, I think you're going to probably see a lot of improvement in that area.

The same thing goes for accounting footnotes. I get accounting footnotes that I have trouble understanding. The reason I have trouble understanding is that the person that wrote it didn't want me to understand it. It's not impossible to write a footnote explaining the four acquisition costs in life insurance or whatever you want to do – you can write it so people can understand it. And if it's written so you can't understand it, I am very suspicious. I won't invest in a company where I can't understand the footnote because I know they don't want me to understand it.

The greater the amount of capital we work with at Berkshire, the worse we are going to do, everything else being equal, in terms of percentage return on equities, and I've been telling our shareholders that for years, and the reason is very simple. When I started out with $10,000, any security in the United States that I could find that would seem cheap could have a very significant impact on that amount of capital. Now if we find something we could put a hundred-million dollars in and we make 50%, that's fifty million pretax; it's about $32.5 million after tax, and that's three-tenths of one percent on that worth.

So it takes very big ideas to have an impact in our universe. Potential investments has shrunk – all businesses that we can buy outright has shrunk as our capital gets greater. We are down to where our universe it very, very small and our returns cannot be as good in the future as in the past. When I started out, I went through Moody's and Standard & Poor's page by page – every page. I just looked at companies, and I found Western Insurance Securities selling at two times earnings, or National America Insurance selling at two times earnings. I found a public utility in New York selling at less than two times earnings. That was just by turning the pages. But I could only put five or ten or fifty thousand dollars in those things. They still had the capacity maybe to double my at-worth or something of the sort, and more than that maybe, but it would be useless for me to do that now at Berkshire. So a lot of money is a drag, but it has other advantages.

QUESTION: I've read that you're not going to burden your children with the fortune that you've amassed. I just wondered, to that extent, could you lend some words of wisdom about family and just planning children, with money?

MR. BUFFET: Well, my general belief is that if you've got a lot of money, that you should probably – and I got this phrase from somebody else – but that you should leave your children enough money so that they could do anything but not enough so that they can do nothing. And I think that there is probably a certain social justice in that. On top of that, I happen to think – it's probably best for development of individuals, although there can be lots of exceptions to that.

I run into people all the time at the country club who say: Isn't it terrible some of these people are on welfare and that they get food stamps and then that just creates a cycle of dependency and then you get second-generation Welfare recipients because they were used to getting the food stamps from their Welfare officer before? And they never stop to think that maybe inherited wealth is really just a lifetime supply of food stamps given through a trust officer instead of a Welfare officer. Did they ever think about the debilitating effect of that, of waking up at age ten seconds and finding out that you never have to work? Compare that to somebody that's probably got a couple of kids that they don't know what to do with and has plenty of problems of their own and are struggling.

And they say, well, we're going to ruin this poor person's desire to work if we give them something that will let them buy a little food.

I personally think that society is responsible for a very significant percentage of what I've earned. I mean, if you stick me down in the middle of Bangladesh or Peru or some place, you'll find out how much this talent is going to produce in the wrong kind of soil. You know, I will be struggling 30 years later. I work in a market system that happens to reward what I do very well – disproportionately well. But Mike Tyson did too. If you can knock a guy out in ten seconds and earn ten million dollars for it, this world will pay a lot for that. If you can bat 360, this world will pay a lot for it. If you're a marvelous teacher this world won't pay a lot for it. If you're a terrific nurse this world will not pay a lot for it.

Now am I going to try to come up with some comparable work system that somehow distributes that? No, I don't think you can do that. But I do think that when you're treated enormously well by this market system, where in effect the rest of society showers goods and service or the ability to buy goods and services on you because of some peculiar talent – you know, maybe your adenoids are a certain way so you can sing – everybody will pay you enormous sums to be on television or whatever. I think society should have a big claim on that. You're lucky enough to be the child of somebody in that position – I think cutting them off with zero is probably a mistake, but I think that setting them up so that essentially they've got this lifetime supply of claims on other people's production of goods and services in society for the rest of their life – it doesn't make much sense to me.

Recommended Readings

•The Anatomy of Success, Nicolas Darvas

• The Dale Carnegie Course on Effective Speaking, Personality Development, and the Art of How to Win Friends & Influence People, Dale Carnegie

• The Law of Success In Sixteen Lessons (Complete, Unabridged), Napoleon Hill

• It Works, R. H. Jarrett

• The Art of Public Speaking (Audio CD), Dale Carnegie

• The Success System That Never Fails (Audio CD), W. Clement Stone

• How I Made $2,000,000 In The Stock Market, Nicolas Darvas

• The Battle for Investment Survival, Gerald M. Loeb

• You Can Still Make It In The Market, Nicolas Darvas

• Technical Analysis of Stock Trends, Robert D. Edwards

Available at www.bnpublishing.net